JUMPSTART TO
POWER
PRAYERS

Never underestimate the power of your prayers.

Blessings,
Marge Gordon

JUMPSTART TO
POWER
PRAYERS

MARJORIE GORDON

Pleasant Word

To my beloved husband, Darrel,
who has encouraged me to develop a variety of gifts
for fifty-one years

Endorsements

JUMPSTART TO POWER PRAYERS

Motivating! Encouraging! Practical! These words describe in part the impact of Marjorie Gordon's new book *Jumpstart to Power Prayers*. What Christian doesn't want a more effective prayer life? The clear step-by-step prayer process that the author outlines will help to produce prayers that pack power. Both historical and personal illustrations are utilized to underscore the validity of each step. As a result of reading this book, I not only want to pray more, but have tools to increase my prayer power.

Warren D. Bullock, D.Min.
Executive Presbyter, General council of the Assemblies of God
Former Dean, School of Ministry,
Northwest University, Kirkland, WA
Adjunct Faculty, Assemblies of God theological Seminary,
and Northwest University
Senior Pastor, Northwest Family Church, Auburn, WA.

Marjorie Gordon has written a practical book using personal examples of the power of effective answered prayer. Through pragmatic use of a notebook during prayer, she displays how prayer can become a vital and essential factor in a strong and overcoming life. The reader will benefit with a deeper faith by putting into use her ideas and actions, which she has tested and proven over a lifetime.

I thought this to be a valuable book. Gordon's emphasis on the use of Scripture in prayer has been something I will strive to use more for greater effectiveness in prayer. *Jumpstart to Power Prayers* has the potential to increase the power of prayer in all of its readers.

John Simpson,
Chaplain (Colonel) U.S. Army, Retired

Jumpstart to Power Prayers is for all those seeking to deepen their prayer lives; a spiritual "pot of gold" at the end of the rainbow.

Author Marjorie Gordon skillfully blends Scripture and personal experiences with quotes and illustrations from the lives of others, then presents a step-by-step guide to the unique method that forever changed the way she prays.

I heartily recommend *Jumpstart to Power Prayers* to anyone who wants a closer relationship with God.

Colleen L. Reece,
Award-winning author/teacher/speaker.
140 "Books You Can Trust"—5 million copies sold.

Gordon pens a colorful and insightful book on prayer. Along with interesting personal testimonies of God's grace and miraculous answers to prayer, Marge outlines a "How-To" manual teaching us how to have "power prayers" in our personal lives. I recommend this book to anyone interested in learning to pray effective and powerful prayers.

Pastor Don Howard
Pastor of Community
Northwest Family Church
Auburn, WA.

Table of Contents

Acknowledgments

I gratefully acknowledge and deeply appreciate the wonderful help that made this book possible. I give special thanks:

- For the persistence of the Holy Spirit Who helped me refine this material for over two decades and prevented me from giving up.
- To my husband, Darrel, for his constant loving support.
- To my mentor and friend Colleen Reece. Without her steady critiques, insight, knowledge, and inspiration, this book would not have been written.
- To my "Seven Sisters" writing group for their thoughtful comments and encouragement.
- To Pastor Warren Bullock, Pastor Don Howard, and Chaplain John Simpson for their careful review of the manuscript and wise input.
- To the many family members, friends, and students from classes and workshops who have shared their experiences.
- To the legacy of those who have gone before us—especially those who took the time to pen a record of God's hand in their lives.

Introduction

Letter to Readers

For years I read stacks of fine books about prayer but I still didn't eagerly and expectantly look forward to praying. My prayers lacked vitality. After I discovered they must be inseparably linked with God's Word, my prayers changed permanently.

My adventure with powerful prayers led me to start keeping a notebook. No, not a book *about* prayer. From my daily Bible reading I collected Scripture prayers, promises, and patterns related to my personal concerns. I found it helpful to divide the growing collection into specific groups. I included dates and names of those for whom I prayed.

Now I pray with tremendous expectation, boldness, and confidence because I'm sure of praying according to God's will and purpose. My prayers are closely connected to God's Word and He promises to watch over His Word to perform it.

Through classes and workshops this material has guided many others to experience the same transforming power by creating their own personal prayer manuals. Unlike a diary or journal, which is replaced annually, your manual will contain a lifetime of prayers and promises gleaned from God's Word and the fellowship of the Holy Spirit. It will become a personal treasury of faith-building answers.

Because accounts of answered prayer have consistently encouraged me, *Jumpstart to Power Prayers* includes numerous examples of God's miraculous intervention in answer to prayer—both mine and others.

I once heard someone say, "If I stopped praying, it wouldn't radically affect my life." Wouldn't it be tragic to live out our lives only to regret not having trusted God more?

I pray this book will be a tool to help individuals and congregations successfully renew their commitment to prayer—the way it has for me.

In Christian love,
Marjorie Gordon

"Prayer is a gift from Almighty God that transforms us, whether we bow our heads in solitude, or offer swift and silent prayers in times of trial. Prayer humbles us by reminding us of our place in creation. Prayer strengthens us by reminding us that God loves and cares for each and every soul in His creation. And prayer blesses us by reminding us that there is a divine plan that stands above all human plans."[1]

—President George W. Bush

CHAPTER ONE

The Power Connection

JAMAICA-BOUND CRISIS

Early morning spring air at the Eugene, Oregon, airport invigorated my husband, Darrel, and me as we unloaded suitcases. Jamaica-bound. Our first perfect, luxury vacation—the expense courtesy of a business award. Our three young children remained at home in the loving care of visiting grandparents.

Once inside the bustling terminal, Darrel left me with the carry-on bags and went to check on seat assignments. Without warning, a wave of nausea and dizziness overwhelmed me. I staggered into a chair and supported my head with a shaking hand. Once before, a horrible case of the flu had attacked me this way.

I held a desperate conversation with God while I waited for Darrel. *God, this thing can't possibly be from You. You have helped us work around so many obstacles to get this far. Help us now. Help me. The Bible, Your Word, holds lots of promises of healing. It says You are my God who heals all my diseases. Lord, I ask You to take these symptoms from me now and remove the cause, in Jesus' precious name.*

I waited, weak and trembling. With no change in my condition, I thought of Jesus' words and continued. *Lord, You said whatever I bind on earth shall be bound in heaven. And You said, "No one can enter a strong man's house and carry off his possessions unless he first ties up the strong man." Help me pray. I don't understand this kind of prayer.*

I silently continued with words I hardly believed were mine. *Satan, I confront you in the name of Jesus. I bind you and command you to take away this dark thing you have brought upon me. I bind you in the name of Jesus and tell you to leave me alone.*

Wow! I'd never prayed a prayer like that before.

Darrel returned and noticed my visible distress. He sat and supported me. "Marge, what's wrong? Do you need to go home?"

"I'm—I'll be okay," I mumbled.

Boarding time. *Lord, what now? I still feel awful.*

Determined to trust God, we boarded and settled ourselves in our seats. Darrel remained worried. "Are you sure you're going to be okay?"

I nodded, but I wasn't sure.

The cheerful flight attendant went through routine safety plans. We were airborne. My condition persisted.

Thirty minutes into the flight I began to improve. Sips of cold orange juice tasted refreshing. Shortly, all my symptoms vanished. I silently thanked God, but I had no idea the extent of His intervention.

Motion sickness had previously afflicted me for hours following any flight. After the long flight to Los Angeles, Miami, and finally Jamaica, I felt great.

Following a wonderfully sunny, relaxing week, the flight home proved equally problem-free. It took a few weeks for me to realize I had been completely delivered of all motion sickness. Previously I couldn't read a map while riding in a car or even sit in a child's swing without experiencing nausea.

I later realized I no longer relied on aspirin several times a week to relieve the frequent headaches I'd had for years. Neither the headaches nor the motion sickness ever reappeared. God had answered my trusting prayers "exceeding abundantly" above all I asked or thought.

THE POWER COLLECTION

Prayer. Wonderful, mysterious prayer. I was eager to pray in this newly discovered power. My encounter en route to Jamaica taught me the value of finding the foundation for my prayers in the Bible. I had read many books *about* prayer. Still, my prayers felt so inadequate. I needed something to guide me daily when I prayed.

In the ensuing months, I kept a notebook near my Bible and added passages of Scripture relating to the needs I prayed about. When the number grew, I put dividers into a three-ring binder and categorized them. Inspired by the biography of George Muller[1] and his lifelong journal of prayers, I added dates and names to the prayers and patterns I collected.

MIGHTY MEN OF GOD PRAY THE WORD

I found confirmation for my growing prayer collection in the examples of two men in the Old Testament who used God's Word in their prayers.

When the children of Israel made a golden calf, God was so angry He told Moses He was going to destroy them all and make Moses into a great nation. Moses pleaded for their lives and concluded: *"Remember Your servants Abraham, Isaac, and Israel, to whom You swore by Your own Self: 'I will make your descendants as numerous as the stars in the sky and I will give your descendants all this land I promised them, and it will be their inheritance forever.'"* Then the Lord relented and did not bring on His people the disaster He had threatened (Genesis 32:13-14).

Moses prayed God's Word.

Nehemiah prayed something similar. He recorded his great distress when he heard reports of the desolation of Jerusalem. After a prayer of confession he continued: *"Remember the instruction You gave Your servant Moses, saying, 'If you are unfaithful, I will scatter you among the nations, but if you return to me and obey my commands, then even if your exiled people are at the farthest horizon, I will gather them from there and bring them to the place I have chosen...'"* (Nehemiah 1:8-9).

Isaiah recorded an invitation from God: "*Review the past for Me, let us argue the matter together*" (Isaiah 43:26).

Jeremiah wrote this powerful message: *The Lord said to me, "You have seen correctly, for I am watching to see that My Word is fulfilled"* (Jeremiah 1:12).

THE FIRST KEY

I knew I had discovered a key confirming my experience. Consistent with these examples, if I want powerful prayers, the kind God delights to answer, they should not only line up with His Word, but may even be His words.

What kind of power is there in God's Word when others speak it? Hear what God told Jeremiah: "*Now, I have put My Words in your mouth. See, today I appoint you over nations and kingdoms to uproot and tear down, to destroy and overthrow, to build and to plant*" (Jeremiah 1:9-10).

The prayers I prayed in the airport had power beyond what I anticipated because I reminded God of His Word—I prayed His Word.

THE SECOND KEY

The second key to the principle of praying God's Word is related to the comforting words in Hebrews 13:8. *Jesus Christ is the same yesterday and today and forever.*

When the Bible reveals the nature of God the Father, Son, or Holy Spirit, we know they remain unchanged. They are the same today for us in the midst of our problems—still willing and able to intervene on our behalf in similar ways.

MORE KEYS TO UNLOCK POWER

My collection of prayer patterns grew daily in direct proportion to my Bible reading. I realized no part of the Bible was off limits after considering the following passages:

- *All Scripture is God-breathed and is useful for teaching, rebuking, correction and training in righteousness, so that the man of God may be thoroughly equipped for every good work (2 Timothy 3:16-17).*
- *For everything that was written in the past was written to teach us, so that through endurance and encouragement of the Scriptures we might have hope (Romans 15:4).*

Each portion of the Bible has something to teach. I look especially for what it teaches about the nature of God, the nature of man, and the relationship between them.

I was sure I was on the right track, but insecurity still undermined my prayers. While I had a great desire to know God's will, I wasn't sure that was possible. How could I pray according to His will? I was overjoyed when I found the words of Colossians 1:9.

For this reason, since the day we heard about you, we have not stopped praying for you and asking God to fill you with the knowledge of His will through all spiritual wisdom and understanding.

God wants us to know His will. Then His will must be revealed in His Word. With that matter settled, I moved on to more confident prayers. God had revealed five keys to powerful prayers:

- All Scripture is inspired by God.
- All Scripture is profitable for instruction.
- Jesus Christ is the same forever.
- We can know His will.
- God watches over His Word to perform it.

In the months that followed my discovery of the relationship of these scripture passages, I developed a growing, life-giving, powerful prayer manual. During this time I had another vivid experience linking the Bible to prayer.

MIDNIGHT CALL

Night wrapped its comforting black velvet cloak around me. I slept peacefully except for the vague awareness that Darrel was on a business trip.

The telephone jangled, shattering my peace. *It's after midnight! Who can this be?*

"Mrs. Gordon, I'm calling from Minneapolis. Your husband has been admitted to the intensive care unit." The nurse spoke in a calm voice. "It appears he has had a heart attack. His condition is stable at this time."

I couldn't focus my thoughts. I groped for a pen. I wrote down the hospital's phone number. The nurse in me fled—the wife panicked. Darrel was 1300 miles from home and I couldn't talk with him. Shock drained my strength. I slid to my knees beside the bed.

"Oh, dear God! Dear Heavenly Father..." I sobbed. After a long while my crying prayers subsided. The deep knowledge of God's faithfulness brought a measure of peace. "Lord, I ask you to heal Darrel. I will trust You in whatever lies ahead."

Even in my confusion, I knew God was in control, trustworthy, and had heard my prayer. I half slept, half prayed through the rest of the night.

The next day I continued to storm heaven and proceeded with the demands of the day. I tried to appear calm until our children were off to school. I frantically considered my options: *Call our pastor? Yes. Try to get a plane reservation to Minneapolis? What about the children? Call the doctor? Yes. That's a good place to start.*

"We have done some blood tests and your husband's condition remains stable. He's resting comfortably. No, he can't come to the phone. No, I can't assure you his condition won't change...." The doctor made no promises except to call me later.

That afternoon I waited in the car for our son David to finish football practice. I removed a small blue New Testament from my purse and held it while I pleaded with God. I opened it randomly and read, *"So I say to you: Ask and it will be given to you; seek and you will find; knock and the door will be opened to you. For everyone who asks receives..."* (Luke 11:9-10).

I stopped. I read the last sentence again. *"For everyone who asks receives."* Then a voice inside spoke clearly. *Marge, you've asked, haven't you?*

"Yes, Lord, you know I have," I cried.

The voice was just as clear as before. *Then what do you think I will do?*

"Oh, Father, You will *heal* Darrel." I accepted the promise and the peace it brought.

Three days later my pale, weak husband arrived home on a plane. His gray countenance revealed how sick he'd been. Further tests by a local cardiologist revealed nothing but a healthy heart. God had surely answered my prayers.

Looking back, I am grateful for the timing of this experience. Both my faith and my prayers had been growing rapidly. It was my daily practice to read the Bible and collect special promises. That undoubtedly explains how I could deal with this crisis without being overcome by fear and anxiety.

Looking Ahead

In the next chapter we will consider the high privilege and responsibility God gives His beloved in calling us to pray. In each of the remaining chapters you will be guided in creating your own personal prayer manual. It will become a collection of Scripture examples and promises, as well as your personal prayers and God's answers. You will discover, as I have, that God cannot open the windows of heaven wide for a person who keeps his Bible closed.

EXAMINE YOURSELF

Stop now and ask yourself these questions. Take time to consider your answers.

1. If I stopped praying how would it affect me? My family? My world?
2. Do my prayers need a transfusion of power?
3. Do I spend more time talking about prayer than I do in praying?
4. Are my prayer intentions noted on random lists and scattered scraps of paper in need of organization?
5. Am I willing to try a new approach to praying with power?

Lord, I am willing and I desire to become an effective intercessor as led by Your Holy Spirit. I ask You to put Your words in my mouth even as You did with Jeremiah, that I might be Your instrument to build and plant, uproot and tear down, destroy and overthrow. Lord, I desire to be a laborer in Your harvest. May Your Kingdom come and Your will be done on earth as it is in heaven. I pray in Jesus' precious name. Amen.

"God binds Himself to His Word. He answers only such prayers as He has promised to answer because they are in harmony with His will."[2]

—Basilea Schlenk

CHAPTER TWO

The Call to Action

STRANDED

Years ago, my husband traded cars with me and took mine in for service. I was often a passenger in his business car but I had not driven it before that cold, windy October morning. After several errands I headed home to Coburg from Eugene, Oregon, on Interstate 5. About three miles from home the motor quit and the car coasted to a stop on the edge of the highway. *Oh no! Out of gas.* The nearest gas station was visible—about a mile away.

High heels sinking in gravel, I staggered my way to the service station. A kind attendant drove me and a full gas can back to the car. When I finally arrived home I breathed a sigh, pleased with my resourcefulness.

That's when I saw it. The car phone. Darrel's business had it installed for him. *Good grief! How could I be so stupid?* By lifting the receiver I could have had gas in five minutes and never left the car.

CALL ON ME

Prayer is like that car phone. There are unlimited resources on the other end of the line, but I must initiate a call. Until we're firmly convinced about the necessity of prayer, we won't be much help to God or ourselves. It's important to lay a solid foundation before beginning a personal prayer manual.

"Call to Me and I will answer you..." (Jeremiah 33:3). Such a simple invitation. It's not only a wonderful privilege, but also a great responsibility. Prayer as God's provision to enable Him to work among us is evident in accounts from the first through the last chapter of the Bible. He has chosen to give us a free will. We can choose to accept or reject Him. We can choose to hear His words or refuse to listen. We can call on Him or not. The decision is clearly ours.

If calling on Him is what He desires of us, we should consider the consequences of not calling. Is it possible we keep people and circumstances from experiencing God's intervention because we have not called on Him?

How can it be that the mighty God of the universe has limited Himself to our call? Because He has created certain rules of order, including free will for mankind, and He won't violate them.

THE BIG PICTURE

Here's the quickest overview you'll ever see of God's delegated power to mankind: God gave dominion over His creation to Adam and Eve. Through careless use of their free will, they submitted their dominion to the serpent (Satan) by giving in to him in the Garden of Eden. Satan tried to subvert Jesus in the same way, in the wilderness. Jesus refused the temptation and bought back the lost rights with His priceless blood on the cross. Now believers are elevated to the position of joint heirs with Jesus and He gives us the authority of His name. Satan is a defeated enemy. Now it's up to us to stand in that victory by inviting God into our affairs—co-operating with Him.

Prayer is God's provision to intervene in the affairs of mankind. When He gave man a free will, He limited His help by our invitation or lack of it. B. J. Wilhite expresses the power of prayer this way: "The Law of prayer is the highest law of the universe—it can overcome the other laws by sanctioning God's intervention. When properly implemented, the law of prayer permits God to exercise His sovereignty in a world under the dominion of a rebel with a free will, in a universe governed by natural law."[1]

JESUS' INVITATION

Jesus not only tells us how important our prayers are, He shows us by His example. We have several accounts of Jesus praying alone, with His disciples, and with large groups. He spent much time in solitary prayer early in the morning and late in the evening. He prayed on mountaintops, in olive groves, and in the darkened garden of Gethsemane. From His heavenly throne He still prays on our behalf.

Jesus called us to pray many times. Consider these passages:

- *"I tell you the truth, My Father will give you whatever you ask in My name. Until now you have not asked for anything in My name. Ask and you will receive, and your joy will be complete"* (John 16:23-24).
- *Then Jesus told His disciples a parable to show them that they should pray and not give up* (Luke 18:1).
- *"Ask and it will be given to you; seek and you will find; knock and the door will be opened to you. For everyone who asks receives; he who seeks finds; and to him who knocks, the door will be opened"* (Matthew 7:7-8).
- *"When you pray, go into your room, close the door and pray to your Father, Who is unseen. Then your Father, Who sees what is done in secret will reward you"* (Matthew 6:6).
- *"I tell you the truth, whatever you bind on earth will be bound in heaven, and whatever you loose on earth will be loosed in heaven. Again, I tell you that if two of you on earth agree about anything you ask for, it will be done for you by my Father in heaven. For where two or three come together in My name, there am I with them"* (Matthew 18:18-20).

Prayers Worth Remembering

The power and importance of prayer is illustrated in several Old Testament records. Abraham's prayers saved his nephew, Lot. Moses obtained mercy for the nation by interceding between the Israelites and God. Elijah's prayers brought fire from heaven to defeat the worshippers of Baal. God gave Hannah a son in answer to her prayers. Daniel's habit of frequent prayers not only raised him to a position of authority but also brought him safely out of the den of hungry lions.

History continues to record men and women who took God seriously and have accomplished miraculous things through prayer.

George Muller's Example

I have been greatly inspired by the book, *George Muller; Man of Faith and Miracles.*[2] Muller lived ninety-three years, from 1805 to 1898. He established several orphanages in England, providing daily for the needs of over 200 orphans. He created the Scriptural Knowledge Institute, which established schools and supported missionaries. It also distributed 281,652 Bibles, 1,448,662 New Testaments, 21,343 copies of the Book of Psalms, and 222,196 other portions of the Holy Scriptures in many languages.[3]

This record becomes more impressive upon discovering that his principles throughout the years were to tell no man of his need, only God, and to never go into debt. Mr. Muller's prayers were grandly rewarded. God provided approximately $7,500,000 for the Scriptural Knowledge Institute.

According to his own words, Muller was an average person and did not have the gift of faith. He read the Bible more than 200 times. He made the discovery that praying without reading the Bible will not provide the same answers as reading, then praying.

Early in his life he recorded in his journal: "Before this time my practice had been, at least for ten years previously, as an habitual thing to give myself to prayer after having dressed myself in the morning. Now I saw that the most important thing I had to do was to give myself to reading of the Word of God, and to meditation on it, that my heart might be comforted, encouraged, warned, reproved."[4]

HUDSON TAYLOR'S PRAYERS OF FAITH

Another Englishman whose life has become a spiritual beacon is Hudson Taylor. Born in 1832, his fruitful life ended in 1905. His most noted achievement was the establishment of the China Inland Mission. (He was inspired by the work of George Muller, who later sent funds for Taylor's ministry in China.)

When Taylor was in medical school preparing to go to China, he wanted to make sure his faith was strong enough for him to embark on the work he felt called to do. "When I get out to China I shall have no claim on anyone for anything. My only claim will be on God. How important to learn, before leaving England, to move man, through God, by prayer alone."[5]

Hudson Taylor had one all-sufficient confidence for the future. If that could fail, it would be better to make the discovery in London than in distant China. In the next two years he experienced many evidences of God's faithfulness.

He once felt moved to give his last coin to a destitute family. He knew unless God supplied, he would go hungry. God's response? He caused a wealthy man to go out late on Saturday night to re-pay a debt, which would become part of Taylor's meager salary. Taylor felt he must not lose the opportunity of further testing the promises of God.

JONATHAN AND ROSALIND GOFORTH

"How hard prayer has been made by man-made rules. Oh, that we could catch a glimpse of the wonders, the power, the easi-ness—yes, the absolute necessity of this God-planned provision, that it might have free course in our lives!"[6] These are the words of Rosalind Goforth who, with her husband, Jonathan, served as a Presbyterian missionary in China from 1888 to 1935. (A book by Hudson Taylor had inspired her.)

Rosalind's own weak faith was often rebuked when she saw the results of the simple, child-like faith of the Chinese Christians. "Li-ming, a warmhearted, earnest evangelist, owned land some miles north of Chang Te Fu. On one occasion, when visiting the place, he found the neighbors all busy placing around their fields little sticks with tiny flags. They believed this would keep the locusts from eating their grain. All urged Li-ming to do the same, and to worship the locust god, or his grain would be destroyed. Li-ming replied: 'I worship the one only true God, and I will pray Him to keep my grain, that you may know that He only is God.'

"The locusts came and ate on all sides of Li-ming's grain, but did not touch his. When Mr. Goforth heard this story he determined to get further proof, so he visited the place for himself, and inquired of Li-ming's heathen neighbors what they knew of the matter. One and all testified that, when the locusts came, their grain was eaten and Li-ming's was not."[7]

AFTER THE KOREAN CONFLICT

In war-torn Korea a young man lay dying of advanced, terminal tuberculosis. The doctors told him he had three or four months to live. He prayed to Buddha but got progressively weaker. Finally, he prayed a prayer that changed his life. "Oh, unknown God, if you exist, please help me. If you can give me my life back, I promise you that I will spend the rest of my days serving you and helping others."[8]

The amazing story of Paul Yonggi Cho's recovery as well as the growth of his ministry is told in dramatic inspired words in *The Fourth Dimension, Volume One*, by Dr. Cho. He is pastor of the Full Gospel Central Church in Seoul, Korea, the largest church in the world. The secret of his spiritual success is often quoted—"I pray and I obey."

SECURE FOUNDATION

God has used biographies of persons I call His superstars to encourage me in prayer and to have a vision for greater answers. The evidence is overwhelming—God still answers prayer!

We know nothing is too large for God to handle, and we know that nothing—and no one—is too small for His tender care. Prayer is a loving conversation between a child and a Heavenly Father. Picturing that relationship helps me when I pray.

Consider the solid foundation on which to build a personal prayer manual: We know God is unchanging. He still watches over His Word to perform it. We know prayer is an essential part of His plan. We can have great influence in the affairs of the world if we align our will with God's.

Someday when we are permitted to see what our prayers have accomplished, may we never experience the anguish of wishing we had prayed more!

PREPARING YOUR PERSONAL PRAYER MANUAL

Your personal prayer manual will be a living, expanding tool. Start with a three-ring binder and 8 ½" x 11" paper. If you get a smaller size you will be disappointed. Trust me. I started with one half that size and quickly outgrew it.

Next, add fourteen divider pages. As you progress through this book, you will personalize a new section at the conclusion of each chapter.

Title the first divider "The Call to Pray." Here you will collect affirmations from your daily Bible reading. Begin with the passages quoted in this chapter. Include examples of prayers that caught your spirit when you read them in the Bible and other sources.

While this section grows it will build your faith to understand the importance of your prayers. We may even be permitted a glimpse of angels poised to bring about the answers to some of our prayers. They, too, listen for the sound of God's Word. *"Praise the Lord, you His angels, you mighty ones who do His bidding, who obey His word"* (Psalms 103:20).

EXAMINE YOURSELF

1. What misconceptions about prayer have been hindering me? About God? About myself?

2. Have I been hoping to hear God's voice yet neglecting to read the Bible?
3. Am I willing to set aside a specific time daily for Bible reading with pen and prayer manual available? (It is better to be faithful to a small commitment than unfaithful to a large one.)

Almighty God, increase my vision for the importance of my prayers. Lead me in Your Word and encourage me to pray boldly. Help me conform my will to Your will, my desires to Yours. I commit the development of my personal prayer manual into Your care. May it be Your instrument to transform me into a mighty intercessor who responds to the sound of Your words. I pray this in the name of my Lord Jesus Christ. Amen.

"Prayer is, and must be, the daily breath of every true disciple! It is not to be a cherished ornament of personal pietism, nor is prayer a spiritual something we keep nearby and use in time of crisis, like a fire extinguisher."[9]

—Gary Bergel

CHAPTER THREE

Get Better Acquainted with God

PRAYER LIMITS

Our prayers are limited by our knowledge of God. Obviously, the greater our concept of God, the greater will be our prayers. Learning to praise God is a perfect way to nurture our ideas about who He is, what He desires, and our relationship with Him. That's why it is important to begin the prayer manual with a section on praise.

The prayers of young children reveal what they know about God. When our granddaughter Holly was three, her prayers were wonderfully simple. "Thank you, Jesus, for the milk, the tuna samiches and the apples. Amen." She understood that everything at lunch had come from Him, even though her mother bought it at the grocery store. She commonly used the names Jesus and God interchangeably. Not bad for a three-year-old. (Remember Jesus' statement that He and the Father are One and if you have seen Him, you have seen the Father?)

PRAISE REWARDS

The foundation for our praise is summed up in Hebrews 11:6: *And without faith it is impossible to please God, because anyone who comes to Him must believe that He exists and that He rewards those who earnestly seek Him.* Earnestly seeking Him is a form of praise.

I recall a time when I was really down in the emotional dumps. For some reason, I gravitated to the piano, sat down and began to play songs from a hymnal. This was no concert, but a one-finger-right-hand, peck-and-play rendition. I sang along with the melodies.

Before long, I grew aware of how much I was enjoying the words and music. I gave up the piano, took the hymnal and relocated to a comfortable chair. I continued to sing softly for more than thirty minutes. When I finally put the book aside, sweet peace had come to replace my depression.

SINGING SCRIPTURE PRAISE

The themes of many songs are lifted directly from the Bible. One of my favorites, "Great is Thy Faithfulness," comes from Lamentations 3:22 RSV: *The steadfast love of the Lord never ceases, His mercies never come to an end; they are new every morning; great is Thy faithfulness.* With words like these filling my mouth and my spirit, depression departed—and stayed gone.

PATTERNS FOR PRAISE

From Genesis through Revelation, a significant portion of the Bible is a record of praise to God. The first recorded praise is after Abraham defeated his enemies. It is spoken by Melchizedek, king of Salem and priest of God: *"Blessed be Abram by God Most High, Creator of heaven and earth. And blessed be God Most High, Who delivered your enemies into your hand." Then Abram gave him a tenth of everything* (Genesis 14:19).

Many accounts in Revelation give glimpses of heavenly praise: *Then I heard what sounded like a great multitude, like the roar of rushing waters and like peals of thunder, shouting: "Hallelujah! For our Lord God Almighty Reigns. Let us rejoice and be glad and give Him glory!"* (Revelation 19:6-7).

Praise scriptures quickly expand our knowledge of God. From just the two selections above we see:

- God is the Creator of heaven and earth (everything).
- He reigns over all.
- He is and will be praised by multitudes in heaven.
- He protects His chosen from the enemy.
- He deserves our gifts.
- He has a representative—a high priest.

SURVEY THE PSALMS

The most generous examples of praise are found in the Psalms, recorded by King David and others. If we studied these examples in journalistic style, we would quickly discover the five "W's" of praise: Who? All people. What? Praise, adoration, and thanksgiving. When? Continually. Where? Anywhere. Why? Because God is worthy to be praised. How? With speaking, singing, musical instruments, and dance. The examples in Psalms cover every circumstance and opportunity for praise.

A GRATEFUL HEART

True praise rises out of a grateful heart, partly because of who God is and partly for what He does. My Aunt Agatha Kruger was quick to praise God for both.

When her husband, Alfred, went to his heavenly home, she was left to dispose of the family farm near Bakersfield, California. Her two grown children helped her choose an attractive mobile home with room for her piano. She brought tubs of azaleas and camellias from the farm and created a colorful, shady garden where she often rested to read her well-worn Bible and talk with her Lord. She lived there comfortably for several years.

After the mobile park was sold, the new owners were neither kind nor friendly. The rent increased. Aggie had difficulty with the upkeep. She considered selling, but many of her neighbors had their coaches for sale, unable to find buyers.

Her nephew offered to rent her a vacant apartment he had bought in a small Christian retirement complex. His offer was so appealing she put her coach on the market and prayed for a buyer.

She had two prospective buyers. Each later backed out. She felt discouraged, but reminded God of His promise in Psalm 57:2: *I will cry unto God Most High; unto God, who fulfills His purpose for me.*

Soon a man called and asked to see the mobile home. When he and his wife arrived, he had a small black book in his hand. He stayed outside to check the exterior while his wife examined the rooms inside. When they completed their inspection, the husband asked many questions and wrote on a list in his black book. Aggie worried. *Lord, this doesn't look very promising.*

He finished his list. "Well, dear, do you like it?"

She smiled. "It has a nice layout. Besides being clean and attractively decorated, it feels so comfortable."

The husband checked his book again. "Nothing's missing. It has everything we want. Mrs. Kruger, We'll take it."

After all the necessary papers were signed, the buyers asked Aggie, "Do you believe in a higher power?"

"Not only do I believe in God," she said, "but He's my constant companion, friend, and guide. Why do you ask?"

"Well, we feel He must have led us to your home," he answered. "It's exactly what we were looking for."

Aggie moved her azaleas and camellias to create a garden arrayed with pink, white and red blossoms at her new apartment. "The answer to my prayer just keeps going," she told me. "Living here at Heritage Village is wonderful. I have fellowship like I have never known before with the other residents who also love the Lord." When she was alone in her apartment she worshiped God while playing her piano. "The hymns fill me with peace and strength."

THE IMPORTANCE OF PRAISE

We should never doubt the importance of praise. Even the prayer Jesus spoke when His disciples asked, "Lord, teach us to pray," begins with praise: *"Our Father in heaven, hallowed be your name..."* (Matthew 6:9).

Hallowed means holy, sacred, revered. God chooses to reveal His nature in His name. He declared His name to Moses as "I Am That I Am." In Scripture He revealed Himself progressively by other names: I Am your Healer, your Provider, your Shepherd, your Righteousness, your Deliverer and your Sanctifier.

THE POWER OF PRAISE

God tells us His ways are not our ways. A graphic illustration of the difference between man's ways and God's is that He defeats enemies in response to praise. One dramatic account is found in the twentieth chapter of 2 Chronicles.

Several tribes had come out to wage war against the Israelites under the leadership of Jehoshaphat. God gives him specific instructions: *"Do not be afraid or discouraged because of this vast army. For the battle is not yours but God's... Go out to face them and the Lord will be with you."*

Jehoshaphat appointed men to sing to the Lord and to praise Him for the splendor of His holiness as they went out ahead of the army, saying: "Give thanks to the Lord for His love endures forever."

As they began to sing and praise, the Lord set ambushes against the men of Ammon and Moab and Mount Seir who were invading Judah, and they were defeated (2 Chronicles 20: selected).

By human logic, that's a ridiculous way to wage war—putting musicians on the front line. But the outcome is clear. When the Israelites demonstrated their faith through their praise, God released His mighty power on their behalf.

IN EVERYTHING GIVE THANKS

When I was first introduced to the need to praise God, I rejected the idea. What kind of egocentric God was this who wanted His subjects to praise Him? It didn't take me long to realize praise is for our benefit. It results in special fellowship with God. According to Psalm 22:3, *He inhabits the praises of Israel.*

We are told to *Rejoice evermore. Pray without ceasing. In everything give thanks: for this is the will of God in Christ Jesus concerning you* (I Thessalonians 5:16-18 KJV).

I tried to practice this advice. One hot summer day, my sixteen-year-old son Larry and I drove home to Clifton Park on the New York Thruway north of Albany. Our Chrysler station wagon motor started coughing and sputtering. We were a quarter of a mile from the next exit ramp, which, unfortunately, was uphill.

"If we can just get to that exit and off the thruway," I said to Larry. We recalled the advice to give thanks in everything so we busied ourselves thanking God. "Thank You, Lord, that You are our Provider. Thank You that You never leave us. We thank You, Lord, even in this malfunctioning car. We know You are in charge."

The distressed motor jerked the car slowly up the exit ramp and died. The car coasted around the corner, to the side of the crossroad and halted. *What now, Lord? Darrel is out of town so we can't call him. Larry still has lots to learn about auto mechanics.*

We walked a block to a gas station—not a service station. The young attendant came and looked under the hood. The radiator was dry. The engine block was seriously over-heated. Our thermostat had failed to warn us. "If you'll walk back to the station with me, I'll give you a large container of water for the radiator," he offered.

Just as we were about to fill the radiator, an older man approached. Dressed in worn blue denim overalls, he was a typical salt-of-the-earth sort. "If you don't want to crack that block, you'd better let it cool an hour or two before you add that water," he advised.

Larry and I listened to him, studied our problem, and decided to take his advice. When we looked up to thank him, he was nowhere in sight—strange in a wooded area nearly void of houses or businesses. We hadn't seen him come and we didn't see him leave.

Later we were able to drive the Chrysler home to Clifton Park. After getting the leaky radiator fixed, replacing our thermostat and burned spark plugs, our faithful station wagon worked just fine. We still wonder how our car could chug and coast uphill and where our mysterious advisor came from then disappeared to so suddenly.

ENTERING IN

When we focus on the unmatchable goodness and faithfulness of God the Father, the Son, and the Holy Spirit, our prayers and expectations increase. Our songs, praise, and thanksgiving usher us into God's presence according to Psalm 100:2,4. *Serve the Lord with gladness: come before His presence with singing. Enter into His gates with thanksgiving and into His courts with praise...*

Praise can flow joyously from the fullness of our hearts or it can be a sacrifice. We are called to praise even when we don't feel like it. *By Him therefore let us offer the sacrifice of praise to God continually, that is, the fruit of our lips giving thanks to His name* (Hebrews 13:15 KJV). *He who sacrifices thank offerings honors Me, and he prepares the way so that I may show him the salvation of God* (Psalm 50:23).

PRAISE SAMPLER

My friend Martha once prayed and fasted a month for some special needs at her church. I asked if she didn't run out of things to pray about.

"I spent the time praying my way through the Psalms," she replied. "There's an amazing amount of inspiration there for personal prayers."

As an exercise in praise, personalize the following selections by speaking them to God using "You" and "Your" and inserting your name where it is appropriate. For example: *O give thanks unto the Lord, for He is good, for His mercy endureth forever* (Psalm 106:1 KJV), can be prayed, "I give thanks to You, Lord, for You are good and Your mercy toward me endures forever."

Take some time to slow down, insert your name and personalize the following passages:

- *I will call upon the Lord who is worthy to be praised: so shall I be saved from mine enemies* (2 Samuel 22:4 KJV).
- *The Lord is my strength and my shield; my heart trusted in Him, and I am helped; therefore my heart greatly rejoiceth, and with my song will I praise Him* (Psalm 28:7 KJV).

45

- *Praise be to the God and Father of our Lord Jesus Christ! In His great mercy He has given us new birth into a living hope through the resurrection of Jesus Christ from the dead, and into an inheritance that can never perish, spoil or fade—kept in heaven for you...*(1 Peter 1:3-4).
- *Blessed is he whose help is the God of Jacob, whose hope is in the Lord his God, the Maker of heaven and earth, the sea, and everything in them—the Lord who remains faithful forever. He upholds the cause of the oppressed and gives food to the hungry. The Lord sets prisoners free, the Lord gives sight to the blind, the Lord lifts up those who are bowed down, the Lord loves the righteous. The Lord watches over the alien and sustains the fatherless and the widow, but He frustrated the ways of the wicked. The Lord reigns forever, your God O Zion for all generations. Praise the Lord* (Psalm 146:5-10).

PREPARING YOUR PERSONAL PRAYER MANUAL

Title the next divider in your notebook "Praise." Add portions of Scripture here as you come across them in your daily Bible reading. You can use those in this chapter as a jumpstart.

If you enjoy organizing, you might want to designate some pages here to separate your collection into themes. These could include God's holiness, His creative acts, His mercy, and His power.

These pages will become a source of refreshing and encouragement. For an interesting and revealing exercise try writing a psalm of your own. I call mine Psalm 151. You can start a list of personal experiences for which you can praise God for His care and intervention.

EXAMINE YOURSELF

1. Complete this sentence: I never realized that praise___
    _____.
2. How would it affect my daily activities if I began each day with praise?
3. List some specific personal reasons to praise God.

4. How can a new focus on praise change my attitude?
5. Think of a means of praise that is new to you, and try it.

Lord, I purpose to spend time daily in praise and thanksgiving because I know it pleases You and benefits me. Continually reveal more of Yourself to me. Holy Spirit, renew my mind and remind me to practice praise. Help me live a life of praise with my words and my actions. Hallowed be your name. I love Your name, Jehovah Shammah, the Lord is There. I thank You that You never leave me. I thank You that You hear and answer my prayers. In Jesus' holy name. Amen.

"Handling dirty linen in the throne room is not accomplished by attempting to hide it, but by openly spreading it before God. That's what confession means: acknowledging exactly what we know to be so."[1]

—Jack Hayford

CHAPTER FOUR

Spiritual Circuit Breakers

DIANE'S DILEMMA

When Diane's daughter, Carrie, was young, Diane was deeply offended by Carrie's Sunday school teacher. She was partially justified in her criticism. Though Diane was a mature Christian, her wounded feelings prevented a right response. She dreaded Sunday mornings and hated taking Carrie to the classroom. She felt terrible, and grew critical of her church.

One Sunday morning she met her friend Susan in the church hallway. "How are you?" Susan asked.

"Not well."

"Neither am I," Susan responded.

"Let's go out to my car and talk," Diane invited.

They talked without revealing names, and realized they were each dealing with a similar problem. Susan's circumstances were different but she, too, had become bitter. Neither wanted to remain that way. Through tears they prayed for one another and sought God's forgiveness.

What happened amazed Diane and Susan. When they finished praying, bitterness was completely gone. They left the car filled with joy and peace.

In subsequent years, Diane watched the young teacher who had offended her become a wonderful woman, beautifully used by the Lord. She marvels that she could ever have seen her any other way.

The teacher later attended a meeting where Diane was the speaker. Several days afterward, Diane received a letter from the young woman expressing how much she loved Diane and had been influenced by her godliness. How grateful the letter made her feel. It further revealed the fruit of her prayer of forgiveness. Forgiveness is like the fragrance a flower gives off when it is crushed.

BARRIERS TO PRAYER

We can block the channel of blessing and communication between God and ourselves with a lack of forgiveness and other offenses. The Bible clearly makes this evident in several passages.

- *But your iniquities have made a separation between you and your God, and your sins have hid His face from you so that He does not hear* (Isaiah 59:2 RSV).
- *He who conceals his sins does not prosper, but whoever confesses and renounces them finds mercy* (Proverbs 28:13).
- *If I had cherished sin in my heart, the Lord would not have listened* (Psalm 66:18).
- *Again and again they turned away and tempted God to kill them, and limited the Holy One of Israel from giving them His blessings* (Psalm 78:41 TLB).

Pogo, a comic strip possum, simplified the problem when he observed, "We have met the enemy and they is us."

No one wants to remain in a position where God won't hear. According to the dictionary, hear includes "to pay attention to, give a formal hearing of, to consent to, to grant."

Electricity coming into our homes provides a good analogy of our problem. The power source flowing to our residence is constant. We enjoy heat, light, hot water, baked chicken, and boiled potatoes as long as nothing interferes with our electricity. When something goes wrong, the circuit breaker disconnects us from the power source. We're upset when the house gets cold, we have to light candles and eat cold food. We immediately call the power company and look for the problem obstructing our power supply.

Unforgiveness and sin block the flow of God's mercy, love, and power to us.

REMOVING THE BARRIERS

Consistent with God's stubborn love, He has provided a way out—a way to re-establish our fellowship with Him. The following scriptures instruct us how to remove the barriers:

- *If we claim to be without sin, we deceive ourselves and the truth is not in us. If we confess our sins, He is faithful and just and will forgive us our sins and purify us from all unrighteousness* (I John 1:8-9).
- *And when you stand praying, if you hold anything against anyone, forgive him, so that your Father in heaven may forgive you your sins* (Mark 11:25-26).
- *In Him we have redemption through His blood, the forgiveness of sins, in accordance with the riches of God's grace that He lavished on us with all wisdom and understanding* (Ephesians 1:7-8).
- *A man who refuses to admit his mistakes can never be successful. But if he confesses and forsakes them, he gets another chance* (Proverbs 28:13 TLB).

The mercy of God is another reason to praise Him. Praise is an important prelude to confession, for we bare our souls and disclose our secrets only to someone we trust. God couldn't make it any easier for us to rid ourselves of the effects of sin and unforgiveness. We recognize it, confess it, and forsake it.

There are those who have trouble believing God makes it so easy. Mercy is when God doesn't give us what we deserve, but He gives us what we don't deserve.

SLANDERED

Several years ago I was asked to accept an office in a Christian women's organization. I needed letters of recommendation, so I requested them from pastors who knew me. Unfortunately, one wrote such a strong letter against me I was given a period of probation instead of the office.

I was stunned. Why would I request a letter from someone who had a bad opinion of me? Our relationship was limited. He was a new young pastor who arrived at our church when my husband and I were preparing to move across the country from New York to Seattle. He observed my strengths as I assumed responsibilities belonging to the head of the house. Darrel was already on the west coast while I was responsible for the activities of our three teenagers as well as the details of the move. Adding to my stress, I had to appear in court with our son David regarding his motorcycle accident. Our other son, Larry, had an appendectomy. One of the criticisms in the letter was that I was not properly submitted to my husband.

Darrel shared my bitterness over the letter. I wasted a lot of time mentally reviewing the slanderous details. After a few days I knew my anger blocked my creativity and cast a shadow over all other relationships. I took the matter to the Lord. "I purpose to forgive this young pastor. I don't feel like forgiving him but I know you require it. Put Your forgiveness into my heart and help me forgive."

I decided that in order to forgive and forget I must stop continually rehearsing the details. This required a lot of effort. In the passing days, I knew God was at work, for the bitterness disappeared.

I later held offices in the organization. My behavior held up under scrutiny, demonstrating the other letters were worthy to be believed. In order to write this account, I asked the Holy Spirit to help me remember details I can now only vaguely recall. Someone has said, "Forgiveness is setting a prisoner free and discovering the prisoner was you."

Spiritual Blinders

We are often dull and unable to recognize our own sins. God has an answer for this problem, too. He sends the Holy Spirit to convict us of sin—not condemn us. None of us can escape the need to confess.

- *All we like sheep have gone astray; we have turned each one to his own way; and the Lord hath laid on Him the iniquity of us all* (Isaiah 53:6 KJV).
- *O God, Thou knowest my foolishness; and my sins are not hid from Thee* (Psalm 69:5 KJV).
- *But how can I ever know what sins are lurking in my heart? Try me and know my thoughts: and see if there be any wicked way in me, and lead me in the way everlasting* (Psalm 139:23-24 KJV).

King David's Folly

The scandalous account of David and Bathsheba is well known. Hollywood even made a movie about their affair. In 2 Samuel chapters 11 and 12, you can read the story and see how the Lord was displeased that David had committed adultery with Uriah's wife and had him killed.

God sent the prophet Nathan to David to confront him with his sin by telling him a parable about a rich man who took a poor man's only ewe. When David didn't recognize himself in the story, Nathan told him bluntly, "You are the man."

The truth struck the king. He confessed, "I have sinned against the Lord."

And Nathan said to David, "The Lord also has put away your sin; you shall not die. Nevertheless, because by this deed you have utterly scorned the Lord, the child that is born to you shall die" (2 Samuel 12:13-14 RSV).

This narrative is a pattern for us. When it is our desire to walk in paths chosen for us by God, He will send His Holy Spirit to convict us if we go astray. When we respond, acknowledge our sins, and determine to discontinue them, we will walk again in God's blessings. Even though God forgives us, there may still be consequences we cannot escape.

DELETED

I used a manual typewriter, then an electric one, long before I acquired a personal computer. I'm still amazed at the ease with which I can handle words. By pressing one key I can delete a word, line, paragraph, or a whole document. With the typewriter, sometimes things were so messed up I just had to start again on a clean sheet of paper.

Fortunately for us, confession and repentance are the keys God provides to clear sins from our record.

- *I've blotted out your sins; they are gone like morning mist at noon! Oh, return to Me, for I have paid the price to set you free* (Isaiah 44:22 TLB).
- *As far as the east is from the west, so far has He removed our transgressions from us* (Psalm 103:12).
- *For I will forgive their wickedness and will remember their sins no more* (Jeremiah 31:34b).

According to these promises, if I wanted to bring up some previously confessed sins, the Lord might well say to me, "Marge, I have chosen not to remember those. They are deleted from your record."

COME CLEAN

Signs often pleasantly surprise me. A carwash in Auburn, Washington, advertised, "Come Clean with Us." God's invitation displayed on a reader-board. A sign on an overgrown yard in Kent, Washington, invited, "Weeds U Pick." The Holy Spirit nudged me. *"I'll point out sins to you. You uproot them, give them up, and let them die."*

Reading accounts in the lives of women in the Sisterhood of Mary, a Lutheran sisterhood, as they rebuilt lives, and a "Land of Canaan" compound in Germany after World War 2 has served to greatly increase my faith. Many stories tell how God intervened in impossible situations, changing human decisions, opening tightly closed doors, protecting and providing for daily needs.

A complex of buildings stands on their grounds as a testimony to God's help in business affairs. They were built and paid for through prayer and faith in God's assistance. The Sisters who worked on the chapel told the following story:

"We had a heavy dump cart which ran on a small track. One day it started skipping off the track, although we were praying in regular shifts in the prayer tent that God would bless and make successful our construction work. It was a troublesome and time-consuming task for the Sisters to get it back on the track each time. This continued to happen until the Sister in charge said, 'We can't go on like this. All of you come into the prayer tent.'

"In the prayer tent we asked God to reveal why He had taken away His blessing. And then it came out that here a Sister was harboring something in her heart against another, or there one had gotten angry with another. One had worked too slow or too fast to suit another, or one had shoveled sand carelessly, or one hadn't cleaned the machine properly. The Sisters had allowed angry judgments and condemnations to creep in and build up tension in our midst. These sins against love stood between us and God and our prayers couldn't go beyond the ceiling.

"Now the painful guilt of these judgments—these sins against love—came to us. We begged forgiveness of one another. We came as poor sinners to God and received afresh His gracious forgiveness. We went back to work—and the dump cart never once jumped the track again."[1]

Another lesson God taught them about unconfessed sin came through downpours of rain. Even when it didn't rain in the nearby city the rain was so constant at their building site that bricks slipped and walls couldn't be erected.

"One day it was raining hard again and we fled into the prayer tent and prayed together. Then suddenly one Sister confessed her sin—her resentment toward God—and said she was to blame for the rain. Others followed. One after another they bowed down in repentance as God's Spirit pointed out their sins. And, behold, when the last one had confessed the rain stopped. This same thing occurred on several occasions. So we experienced something of the truth of this scripture: *I would send rain upon one city and send no rain upon another city; one field would be rained upon and that field on which it did not rain withered* (Amos 4:7).[2]

The two masons working with them who observed all this failed to worry about the threat of rain thereafter. At the first drops of rain they would say to one another, "Relax. As soon as the Sisters get together in the tent, it'll stop."[3]

Personal Prayer Manual

Scriptures in this chapter make a good beginning for the next section of your personal prayer manual. Title the divider "Barriers." Leave room to add other scriptures you discover in your daily Bible reading.

On a separate page begin a list of things you know need confessing and forgiveness. Use a red pen. Invite the Holy Spirit to bring things to your attention. You may need to pray, "Lord, help me be willing to relinquish these to You."

After you have honestly dealt with each item, take a red felt pen and cross boldly through it. This will be a reminder it is only through the blood of Jesus our sins are forgiven. "*If we walk in the light, as He is in the light, we have fellowship with one another, and the blood of Jesus, His Son, purifies us from every sin* (1 John 1:7). If you used a red pen, your confession will be nearly invisible—a reminder you needn't waste time praying over this again. It is gone like the morning mist at noon.

I have added the following list into my prayer manual. It is supposedly derived from notes by John Wesley. True or not, it's a good confession starter.

Father, forgive me as I forgive those who sin against me. Forgive me for:

- Consciously or unconsciously creating the impression I am better than others, being proud.
- Being dishonest in any of my acts and words or exaggerating.
- Being untrustworthy.
- Being a slave to dress, friends, work or habits.
- Being self-conscious, self-pitying, or self-justifying.
- Not letting the Bible live in me today.
- Not allowing time for the Bible to speak to me every day.
- Not speaking to someone else about my faith.
- Not praying about the money I spend.
- Not getting to bed on time and not getting up on time.
- Disobeying God in anything.
- Doing something about which my conscience is uneasy.
- Being defeated in any part of my life.
- Being jealous, impure, critical, irritable, touchy or distrustful.
- Wasting my spare time.
- Fearing, disliking, disowning, holding resentment toward or disregarding anyone.
- Grumbling and complaining.
- Being undisciplined.
- Being judgmental.
- Idle words I have spoken.
- Compromising and making friends with the world.
- Being in debt.

That's quite a list. Let the Holy Spirit be your guide as you check up on yourself.

EXAMINE YOURSELF

1. Am I guilty of presenting my want list before coming clean with God?

2. What is the best time of day for prayers of confession? Evening? Morning? Other? Why?
3. Review your activities today—hour-by-hour—the people, work and leisure. Invite the Holy Spirit to give you conviction for every offense committed or received.
4. Are you ready to be accountable?

Holy Father, thank You for removing the penalty for my sins. Perfect Lamb of God, I thank You for shedding Your precious blood that covers all my unrighteousness. I purpose to walk in forgiveness today, that my sins may be forgiven according to Your Word. Holy Spirit, fellowship with me and help me listen for Your guidance. Show me my sins that I may repent and not repeat them. I pray in the powerful name of Jesus. Amen.

"There is also such a thing as negative imaging. And the most common name for it is worry…. 'Trust God' the Bible keeps saying, because the more you trust the less you have to worry about."[4]

—Dr. Norman Vincent Peale

CHAPTER FIVE

Personal Growth

In Training

It may seem selfish to devote a chapter to our personal needs so near the beginning of the prayer manual. It's actually just the opposite. Our prayers for others are limited by our spiritual maturity. When we grow in Christ-likeness by bringing our lives into obedience to God's will and His Word, we will pray more effectively for others.

A military recruit doesn't grab a gun and head for the nearest war. He trains his body to withstand physical hardships, learns to use weapons and learns obedience to his commanding officer. Then he's a useful member of the armed forces wherever he's needed. So it is with prayer warriors under the Commander-in-Chief of all of heaven's armies.

Our Provider

It's important to understand that God wants us to pray about our daily needs. He delights in supplying when our requests are in line with His will: *Ask and it will be given you; seek and you will find; knock and the door will be opened to you. For everyone who asks receives; he who seeks finds; and to him who knocks, the door will be opened.*

Which of you, if his son asks for bread, will give him a stone? Or if he asks for a fish, will give him a snake? If you, then, though you are evil, know how to give good gifts to your children, how much more will your Father in heaven give good gifts to those who ask Him (Matthew 7:7-11)!

Fortunately, God loves us as His children and meets us where we are. New babes in Christ, knowing little about prayer, needn't be intimidated. He specifically invites us to come as little children.

When my granddaughter Jenny was tiny, she learned she'd get picked up if she just extended her arms. Later, when her talk was charming babbling sounds, we responded for the ones she used for bottle and pacifier. We didn't care if she used the right words. At age three, her conversations were long, her requests more extensive. She got both "yes" and "no" answers because her judgment was still that of a toddler. It's reassuring to know God loves and cares for us even more than we love our family.

The four gospels present many examples revealing how God supplies our needs. For the hungry, Jesus multiplied a few fish and loaves of bread to feed thousands. To pay taxes, He provided money through a miracle when Peter did as he was trained—he went fishing. Jesus met business needs when He provided an overflowing catch of fish to weary fishermen. He showed us the need to feed our spirits in the conversation with Martha when she asked Him to send Mary to the kitchen to help her. He healed the sick, cast out demons, and even restored life to some already dead.

BE SPECIFIC

Seasoned prayer warriors testify to the need to state our requests specifically—not in vague generalities. When we pray details, we will easily recognize God's answer.

Dr. Paul Yonggi Cho relates an experience early in his Christian life that changed his prayers. When God healed him of terminal tuberculosis, Cho kept his promise to serve God. He lived in a bare, unheated room and had little to eat. Yet people were coming to know Christ in Cho's little tent church.

He taught the people that they could have confidence in God to meet their needs. He prayed for his few necessities—a desk, a chair, and a bicycle. After months passed, he became discouraged when these needs went unmet. He cried to God and experienced God's peace.

"I got very quiet and began to listen. As I settled my emotions and opened my spiritual ears, I heard the still, small voice of God. *'My son, I heard your prayer when you first prayed four months ago.'*

" 'So where,' I yelled out, 'is my answer?'

"'Your trouble, my son, is that you do what so many of my children do. When you give Me your requests, they are so vague that I cannot answer them. Don't you realize there are dozens of chairs, many kinds of desks of differing woods, and many makes of bicycles? Why aren't you more specific?'

"This was the turning point of my life. Now I had the keys to getting my prayers answered…'Now, what should I ask for specifically?' I asked myself. Then I prayed, 'Heavenly Father, I would like to have a desk made out of Philippine mahogany. My desk is going to be large enough for me to be able to lay out all of my study books along with my Bible…I would like a chair with a steel frame so that it is sturdy and has little wheels…Father, the bicycle is to be one made in the U.S.A.'"[1]

He learned that prayers, like fertile eggs, sometimes need to incubate. After several months he receive all three items exactly as he had described them.

Lorrie, a student in my class, told how God provided her family with their daily bread. "During a time when we had little money, we ran out of food. A neighbor who worked for a dairy began bringing us milk, eggs, and ice cream. One morning my husband and I worried over the desperate clothing needs of our youngest child, Hannah. About two hours later someone I'd never seen came to my door and handed me a bag of clothes. Examining them, I realized they would fit Hannah perfectly. The Lord must have heard the cry of my heart, because I hadn't even prayed yet."

Gideon and his fleece provide an outstanding example of how God honors specific prayers. Not only did he request that the fleece be wet while the surrounding earth was dry, he reversed his request that the fleece be dry and the ground wet. (See Judges 6). Gideon made sure there was no confusion that he was dealing with God.

From *The Kneeling Christian* comes this challenge: "If God were to answer the words repeated on our knees this morning, should we know it? Should we recognize the answer? Do we even remember what we asked for?"[2]

THE HELPER

Because He helps us pray, the importance of our fellowship with the Holy Spirit cannot be exaggerated. We are commanded to live in the Spirit and walk in the Spirit.

Dr. Cho stresses the significance of this constant relationship. "We are joined with the Holy Spirit when we receive Jesus Christ as our personal Savior; therefore we can no longer consider ourselves as individuals apart from the Holy Spirit.... I like to think of our relationship with the Holy Spirit in very practical terms: We are actually living with the Holy Spirit, sleeping together, awakening together, eating together, doing our work together and praying together.

"If we don't maintain this consciousness of being together with the Holy Spirit, then our work is empty and unfulfilled."[3]

Unless we invite the Holy Spirit to help us pray, we are as foolish as a four-year-old who tries to fix his broken bike without asking for help.

The scene in 2 Kings 19:14-20 inspires me: Hezekiah, king of Judah, had come under the threat of attack by the king of Assyria. He received a letter from the enemy predicting his defeat. "*Then he went up to the temple of the Lord and spread it out before the Lord, and he prayed to the Lord....*" It's as if he arranged a conference and said, "Okay, God, what are we going to do about this?"

I have used this example several times to bring a pressing problem to the Lord for His counsel. I equip myself with my Bible, a large pad of paper, and a pen. I ask, "Holy Spirit, help me work through this problem." I write all the thoughts that follow.

Mundane Problems: Godly Solutions

A confusing time occurred shortly after our family moved to Seattle several years ago. My list began: Bare windows need drapes; twenty-fifth wedding anniversary in three weeks; time for writing... Next I wrote the thoughts that came. *Order ready-made drapes from a catalogue. Delay anniversary celebration two weeks. Write every morning after the children go to school. Use the afternoons for homemaking demands.*

The answers brought peace. I knew I had the fellowship of the Holy Spirit. Other times I have repeated this approach with sticky problems, always with practical solutions. Once the response was, *"Arise at five a.m. and write for two hours before the family gets up."* I wasn't thrilled with this thought. I prayed, "Since this is Your idea, Lord, I'll depend on Your help to get me out of bed." This became my most productive writing experience ever.

Our Business: God's Business

When Hope Traver's husband started his surgical practice in 1929 they were quite poor. She charged the equivalent of two weeks' wages for two new uniforms at a uniform shop. On the way home she went into a dime store. She placed the package of uniforms on the counter when she paid for her purchase. When she turned to leave it was missing. She explained the problem to the manager, who did nothing about it.

The uniform shop gave her assurance that her address was on the package and it might show up. After a week, her husband said, "Hope, you will have to buy more uniforms." With a heavy heart she prepared to leave. The doorbell rang. When she opened the door a stranger handed her a package she had found under a park bench.

Hope examined the package and was amazed that it was dry. There had been a heavy snow the day before, yet the uniforms were in perfect condition.

Through the many years Hope walked in the Spirit, this provision served as a reminder of how much God cared about all the details of her life.

GOD'S CLOCK

In David Wilkerson's book, *Beyond the Cross and The Switch-blade*, he devoted an entire chapter to "Holy Ghost Timing." "It took me years to discover the premier lesson that God has a timing all His own, and that I must not be impatient when His timing doesn't coincide with mine."[4]

Cindy and Jim learned God's timing is best. They were both members of a U.S. Air Force flying squadron. Married, they couldn't fly on the same crew, so they rarely had the same schedule. He spent his week on twenty-four hour alert just when she finished. Having leave time together was almost impossible.

Cindy still had fifteen months of active duty. Because they both wanted children, they prayed God would bless them with a baby. Cindy planned to finish her time with the Air Force after the baby's arrival.

After eight months of being unable to conceive, they were given an unusual one-week leave together—a rare time to relax and enjoy each other. Seven months later Cindy finished her time in the service. Two months afterward she gave birth to a healthy son. In the interim two months she accompanied Jim to California for his six-week training program.

The Persian Gulf conflict began the week after their baby arrived. Jim was later sent to Europe to provide air support. Two days before the intensive ground war began, he received the unexpected assignment to fly a damaged plane back to the U.S. for repairs.

Looking back, they appreciated God's perfect timing. If their baby had arrived on their schedule, Cindy might well have been sent to the Persian Gulf after her maternity leave.

THE FAMILY WAGON

God shows His love for families in unique ways. Our family needed a van for a cross-country trip to help Darrel's parents celebrate their golden wedding anniversary. After our move to Schenectady, New York, in 1976 we set aside $5,000 for a van. We asked God to help us, and then looked everywhere. With two tall teen-age boys, a pre-teen daughter, and a German shepherd, we really needed the extra space a van would provide—but what we needed didn't seem to exist.

One afternoon, on our way to watch a high-school baseball game, we took a wrong turn. Before we found our directions, we saw a large blue and white Dodge van with a For Sale sign in the window parked in a yard. We got out and looked it over. It had much more than we had prayed for. It was almost a mini-motor home. A raised roof made space for a double bed to be pulled into place. The middle bench seat could be reversed to face the rear seat, forming a dinette when a table was put in place. It had a small refrigerator, sink, and even a closet with a port-a-potty bathroom. A beautiful van, but surely beyond our budget.

The price? $5,000. The owner had just parked it there one hour before, and he planned to advertise it in the paper the following day. We bought it and enjoyed it for fifteen years. Our 7,000-mile round-trip to California in our Family Wagon became a time of joyful memories for the entire family. We thanked God many times for this provision.

SWEET THINGS

I recall a time when my spiritual needs and my bodily appetite wrestled. Every time I decided to bring my appetite under control, I had a tremendous urge to search the cupboards for something sweet. Then in my daily reading I found Psalm 119:103. *How sweet are thy words unto my taste! Yea, sweeter than honey to my mouth* (KJV).

Thinking of Psalm 19, verses 7-10, I turned and read how the laws, precepts, commandments, and judgments of the Lord are not only perfect, sure, and right, but they are *sweeter also than honey and the honeycomb.*

I prayed, "Lord, whenever I'm tempted to yield to my sweet tooth, I will go to the Bible and let You fill me with the honey of Your Word." Whenever I followed this pattern I forgot about looking in the cupboards. No area of our lives is off-limits for God's loving concern and provision.

Patterns

In my personal prayer manual there are seven passages of Scripture that have ongoing significance in my daily walk. Each helps me progress in my walk in the Spirit.

- *Create in me a pure heart, O God, and renew a steadfast spirit within me (Psalm 51:10).*
- *Set a guard over my mouth, O Lord; keep watch over the door of my lips. Let not my heart be drawn to what is evil…(Psalm 141:5).*
- *Commit thy way unto the Lord; trust also in Him and He shall bring it to pass (Psalm 37:5 KJV).*
- *Trust in the Lord with all thine heart, and lean not unto thine own understanding. In all thy ways acknowledge Him, and He shall direct thy paths (Proverbs 3:5-6 KJV).*
- *If any of you lacks wisdom, he should ask God, Who gives generously to all without finding fault, and it will be given to him (James 1:5).*
- *But when the Holy Spirit controls our lives He will produce this kind of fruit in us: Love, joy, peace, patience, kindness, goodness, faithfulness, gentleness, self-control; and here there is no conflict with Jewish laws (Galatians 5:22 TLB).*
- *But He said to me, "My grace is sufficient for you, for My power is made perfect in weakness." Therefore I will boast all the more gladly about my weakness so that Christ's power may rest on me (2 Corinthians 12:9).*

I have collected many scriptures with personal significance as they relate to a specific need or problem.

Your Personal Prayer Manual

Title the fourth divider "Daily Walk." The scriptures in this chapter are a great jumpstart. Depend on the Holy Spirit to help you pray for your own needs. Always keep your prayer manual nearby when you read your Bible. The Holy Spirit will often use your reading to give you direction and encouragement.

Ask God to show you His plan in your circumstances. Be prepared to write down ideas that come. My written prayers encourage me in the future. When I read them later I often pray, "Lord, I'm still trusting You with this." Make it a habit to put a date near each new entry. Your faith will increase as you date the answer to each prayer. These pages will become a combination of personal prayers and Scripture patterns.

EXAMINE YOURSELF

1. How much have I brought God into my thinking, planning, and activities today?
2. Have I asked God to help me identify and develop my gifts and talents?
3. Can I accept constructive criticism and use it for personal growth without resenting it?
4. Have I asked God to help me set goals? With the Holy Spirit's help, write one long-term goal, one mid-term goal, and one short-term goal.
5. If someone looked for Christ in me would they be disappointed?

Heavenly Father, I truly desire to grow in Christ-likeness. Open my eyes to see myself as You see me. Open my ears to hear my words as You and others hear them. Holy Spirit, fellowship with me as I use the Scriptures to measure my growth. Lead, guide, and direct me in my daily walk. In the blessed name of Jesus I pray. Amen.

"True community rests on mutual thought, mutual labor, and mutual prayer, the whole affair being held in God's light and grace. Suppose nobody asked God's help, and therefore drew no goodness from the Source of Goodness. Suppose everybody quit thinking about his neighbor. Suppose everybody quit working for other people. Yes, we should complete that "suppose;" suppose everybody quit praying for anybody."[5]

—George A Buttrick

CHAPTER SIX

Called to Intercede

UNLIMITED POSSIBILITIES

When I ask myself, "What have I done today that has eternal value?" there is one sure answer: *I prayed for someone.*

"God has a wonderful plan by which you can have worldwide influence…. Through prayer you can accompany any missionary to remote reaches of the earth…feed millions of starving men, women and children hungry for bread for their bodies and for the Bread of Life.

"Through prayer you can contribute to the ministry of any pastor or evangelist … anywhere in the world. Through prayer you can take a suffering infant in your arms. Through prayer you can touch a fevered brow in any hospital, mediating the healing love of Jesus."[1] These words of Wesley Duewel reveal the unlimited possibilities of intercession.

Let's examine the call to intercession. It provides the foundation for the remainder of your personal prayer manual. The dictionary defines intercede: To plead or make a request on behalf of another or others, to intervene for the purpose of producing agreement.

One who intercedes takes the role of mediator. According to 1 Timothy 2, Jesus is the only mediator between God and man.

How, then, can we be intercessors? Because we have been made *co-heirs with Christ* (Romans 8:17) and we are *a chosen people, a royal priesthood* (1 Peter 2:9).

In his book *Destined for the Throne*, Paul Billheimer offers many refreshing insights about the role and importance of our prayers of intercession. "This world is a laboratory in which those destined for the throne are learning, by actual practice in the prayer closet, how to overcome Satan and his hierarchy. God designed the program of prayer as an 'apprenticeship' for eternal sovereignty with Christ. We are learning the 'trick of the tools'—how to use the weapons of prayer and faith in overcoming and enforcing Christ's victory so dearly bought. What foes will be left to overcome in the eternal ages we do not know. But the character acquired in overcoming here will evidently be needed when we have joined the Bridegroom on His throne. *'To him that overcometh will I grant to sit with me in my throne'* (Revelations 3:21 KJV).... The prayer closet is the arena which produces the overcomer."[2]

PATTERNS AND PROMISES

When we consider scriptures about intercessory prayer, we discover more than an invitation. We discover a command. If we are ever tempted to shrug off our responsibility to pray with a spiritual sounding phrase like, "I don't feel called to intercessory prayer," the following scriptures dismiss that argument.

- *But I say unto you, love your enemies, bless them that curse you, do good to them that hate you, and pray for them which despitefully use you, and persecute you; that ye may be the children of your Father which is in heaven* (Matthew 5:44-45a KJV).
- *I urge, then, first of all, that requests, prayers, intercession and thanksgiving be made for everyone—for kings and all those in authority, that we may live peaceful and quiet lives in all godliness and holiness* (1 Timothy 2:1-2).

- *And pray in the Spirit on all occasions with all kinds of prayers and requests. With this in mind, be alert and always keep on praying for all the saints (Ephesians 6:18).*
- *For this reason, since the day we heard about you, we have not stopped praying for you and asking God to fill you with the knowledge of His will through all spiritual wisdom and understanding. And we pray this in order that you may live a life worthy of the Lord and may please Him in every way: bearing fruit in every good work, growing in the knowledge of God…(Colossians1:9-10).*
- *As for me, far be it from me that I should sin against the Lord by failing to pray for you. And I will teach you the way that is good and right (1 Samuel 12:23).*
- *And the Lord turned the captivity of Job, when he prayed for his friends; also the Lord gave Job twice as much as he had before (Job 42:10 KJV).*

These passages make clear the responsibility and blessings of intercessory prayer.

NEVER TOO YOUNG

Corrie ten Boom, in her book, *In My Father's House*, tells how, at the age of five, her mother led her to invite Jesus into her heart. Her mother explained to her, "Now, Corrie, you are an intercessor." Jesus became very real to Corrie. She remembers praying for all her neighbors and the poor drunks she saw being pushed into the jail near her house.

Years later, after Corrie survived imprisonment in a Nazi concentration camp, she became well known as a speaker and evangelist. Often people came to Corrie after a speaking engagement and told her they or their parents had lived in her neighborhood, and how they came to receive Jesus as their Savior. Once Corrie received this testimony from a man she had prayed for seventy-six years before.[3] What power—prayer from a 5-year-old intercessor!

This tender story inspired me when my granddaughter Holly was five. We, too, had a precious conversation where Holly invited

Jesus into her heart. I told her, "Holly, now you're an intercessor," and explained what that meant. She accepted her new role with serious faith. She even prayed about problems over the telephone.

When Holly was in the first grade she told me a wonderful story. "I told some kids in my class I was an intercessor and if they wanted to know more I would meet them later on the playground. Five girls and one boy came to talk so I told them, 'Jesus lives in my heart and He will hear my prayers.' One of the girls asked me to pray for her mother and father because they were getting a divorce. Grandma, I felt like a grown-up when I prayed for her."

What a great heritage we can pass along when we understand the precious call to be an intercessor!

AGE IS GOOD

The Bible gives us a glimpse of an elderly intercessor. When the infant Jesus was presented in the temple, an 84 year-old woman named Anna gave thanks to God and spoke prophetically of the child. Anna was well known in the temple, for *she never left the temple, but worshipped night and day, fasting and praying* (Luke 2:36-37).

When I had three active children at home, I was busy just keeping everyone fed, clothed, and organized. I remember how little time I had for prayer. Now that my home is quiet and less demanding, I count it a blessing and a responsibility to bring my family daily before the Lord.

I encourage young parents, "Ask older Christians to pray for you, especially if there are no praying grandparents in your family."

THE SHADOW OF OUR PRAYERS

Our prayers can cast long shadows, touching where we cannot. I received a letter from my friend Brenda so different from her usual upbeat style. "I don't know what has come over me. I seem to spend an incredible amount of time sleeping. I'm even passing up tennis dates, something that usually gets me enthused." She referred to ongoing alcohol problems with her husband and behavior problems with a son. She had moved from my city to another state. I grieved for her.

When my weekly Bible study/prayer group met, I asked them to help me pray for Brenda. Listening for the leading of the Holy Spirit, we prayed several general prayers for help and healing. Then someone spoke with authority, "Satan, we bind you and command you to take every dark, unclean thing away from Brenda now. She's God's property. We command this in the name of Jesus. Lord Jesus, refill Brenda with your peace, light, love, and health."

When I later talked to her on the phone, Brenda told me how she had become suddenly free from the sleep problem and able once again to tackle life with her usual vigor. What great encouragement for my prayer partners and me.

SOMETHING GREATER

When President George H.W. Bush gave his State of the Nation address on January 29, 1991, he said something to the citizens of the United States that caught my imagination. He said, *"We are a part of something larger than ourselves."*

Yes, that's true. This nation stands for ideals known around the world. But my thoughts went beyond that implication. Christians are part of something larger than themselves—and intercessory prayer is our key to participate in a power and plan much greater than the limits of our humanity.

Paul Billheimer likens it to the keys of a safe deposit box. The banker has one key and we have another key. Neither works without the other. "Heaven holds the key by which decisions governing earthly affairs are made but we hold the key by which those decisions are implemented…. Prayer is not overcoming reluctance in God…. The content of all true prayers originates in the heart of God. So it is He who inspires the prayer in the heart of man, and the answer to every God-inspired petition is already prepared before the prayer is uttered. When we are convinced of this, then faith for the answer is easy—far easier than it would be otherwise."[4]

I believe God desires us to talk more with Him about others than to talk with others about Him. We must each discover whose lives are entrusted to our prayers.

TUNE IN

An important step in intercession is to develop a listening ear. When we ask God to make us aware of His desires, we must learn to trust the thoughts that follow. There may also be an urging from the Holy Spirit Who will draw us into deep prayer for a specific reason.

Newspapers and news broadcasts provide prayer starters. I pray whenever I hear a siren because I once worked on a volunteer ambulance crew. When an airplane flies overhead, a friend prays for its occupants. If I don't know how else to pray, I say, "Lord, may Your Kingdom come and Your will be done in that person's life and circumstance." I know that's praying His will.

YOUR PERSONAL PRAYER MANUAL

Label the fifth divider "Called to Intercede." Here you'll compile a list of scriptures inviting intercessory prayer and examples of the results of prayers for others.

The remainder of the prayer manual will be devoted to specific areas of intercession—family, nation, church, etc. Until we explore these other areas, begin accumulating related scriptures and prayers here, adding extra pages to be relocated later.

EXAMINE YOURSELF

1. Do I care about the people in my home, my workplace, and my neighborhood enough to pray for them?
2. Do I spend more time gossiping with others than talking with God about others?
3. Do I ask the Holy Spirit to bring prayer needs to my mind?
4. Do I read or listen to the news with thoughts of praying for people and nations in crisis?

5. On a scale of 1 to 5, (5 being super), rate yourself as an intercessor. Is it time to plan my prayers for others so I will be more dependable and effective?

Dear Heavenly Father,

"Thank You for teaching me through Your Word that I am to be an intercessor-priest of God. Thank You for giving me permanent access to You at any time through prayer, and for calling me now to be a warrior for You in Your army of intercessors....

"Teach me, Lord, to see the world through Your eyes, to love the world with Your love, to weep with You over the sorrows and sins of the world. I am unworthy to carry prayer burdens, but I am willing to share them with You. I know not how to prevail in prayer. Teach me, Lord, to prevail.

"Teach me how to discipline my life so that I take time to intercede. Teach me to have a listening ear so I can discern Your prayer assignments for me. Let my heart share something of Your longings and tears as I intercede. Empower me by your Holy Spirit to believe and stand on Your promises. Empower me to be strong in prayer warfare, to withstand the powers of darkness and to drive them back by the authority of Your name....

May my worship, my love in prayer, my hidden intercession bring joy to Your heart, victories in Your cause according to Your will, and glory to Your name....

"In Your name I pray, Jesus, My wonderful Lord."[5]

"Reading the Scriptures makes us aware that prayer is asking and receiving. It is like sitting at a family meal and asking, "Please pass the potatoes." No pleading is necessary. The provision was made when the potatoes were put on the table…. Prayer is asking for God's provision to be passed to our place."[6]

—Judson Cornwall

CHAPTER SEVEN

Standing in the Generation Gap

God's Family Plan

Families established according to God's design are the recipients of God's great blessings and covenants. The Bible contains a multitude of examples of how God's loving relationship with one family member is responsible for the protection and preservation of the entire family. Looking at some of these inspires our faith so we will want to effectively stand in the gap for our own families.

Patterns of Family Favor

Noah found favor in the eyes of the Lord. God chose him for the long and difficult task of building an ark. God spoke to him, *But I will establish My covenant with you, and you will enter the ark—you and your sons and your wife and your sons' wives with you* (Genesis 6:18). Noah's entire family was saved in the flood that covered the earth, annihilating the remainder of that wicked generation.

Abraham's children were included in the promises God made to him. God made several covenants with Abraham, summed up in this one: *I will establish My covenant as an everlasting covenant between Me and you and your descendants after you for the generations to come, to be your God and the God of your descendants after you* (Genesis 17:7).

Because Rahab protected the Israelite spies, she and her family were saved when the city of Jericho fell into the hands of the Israelites.

Cornelius, a Roman centurion, called together his relatives and close friends when he knew Peter was coming—according to God's command. Peter told them the account of Jesus' life, teachings and death. *While Peter was still speaking these words, the Holy Spirit came on all who heard the message. The circumcised believers who had come with Peter were astonished that the gift of the Holy Spirit had been poured out even on the gentiles. For they heard them speaking in tongues and praising God* (Acts 10:44-46). Even Cornelius's extended family and friends received this blessing because he and his family were devout and God-fearing.

When a miraculous earthquake opened prison doors and released prisoners' chains, Paul and Silas spoke comfort to the jailer who was about to kill himself. *Believe in the Lord Jesus, and you will be saved—you and your household* (Acts 16:31). What encouraging words, not only to the jailer, but also to subsequent generations who continue to read them.

THE CHRISTIAN FAMILY

Many fine books examine closely the roles and responsibilities God places within Christian families. It's not the purpose of this chapter to elaborate on those but the additional information gleaned will enhance prayers for family members.

LEGACY OF PRAYER

I heard Dr. Bill Bright, the founder of Campus Crusade for Christ, give his testimony. He added, "My mother's prayers caught up with me."

I suspect a survey of Christians would yield high numbers confirming the important role the prayers of mothers, grandmothers, fathers, and grandfathers played in their lives. Paul wrote to

Timothy, *I have been reminded of your sincere faith, which first lived in your grandmother Lois and in your mother Eunice and, I am persuaded, now lives in you also"* (2 Timothy 1:5).

GRANDMA'S PRAYERS

My Grandmother Henrietta Theimer Kruger came from Germany as a teenager and never learned to read English. I remember her well-worn black German Bible on the table near her wicker rocking chair. When I was fortunate to eat potato pancakes with honey or another of the special treats at her table, I wondered at her prayers of blessing. Always spoken in German—though she did speak English with a heavy accent—they were filled with emotion. She always wiped tears from her eyes afterward.

My heart has always been tender toward God, though I walked at a distance through my college years. Someday in heaven I expect to learn how I was protected and drawn to God as a result of Grandma's prayers.

UMBRELLA PRAYERS

I pray two kinds of prayers for my family. Some are umbrella-like in nature—a covering for mature growth and protection. Others are for specific needs as problems arise.

In the book of Job, we read of a hedge of protection provided by God. *"Does Job fear God for nothing?"* Satan replied. *"Have you not put a hedge around him and his household and everything he has?"*... (Job 1:9-10).

Another covering prayer I like is based on growing in Christ and in love: *This is what I have asked God for you, that you will be encouraged and knit together with strong ties of love, and that you will have the rich experience of knowing Christ with real certainty and clear understanding* (Colossians 2:2 TLB).

It's never too soon to put the preparation and selection of a lifetime mate for our children into God's hands. Encouraged by Proverbs 19:14, I did this before the teen years arrived. *A father can give his sons homes and riches, but only the Lord can give them understanding wives* (TLB).

The Blood Covering

Our friend Doug Selberg tells us he and his wife take seriously the responsibility of praying a covering of the protecting blood of Jesus over their family daily.

One morning they felt an urgency to pray an extra covering over their two grandsons, ages one and three. That night their daughter called to tell them, "Keith's guardian angels sure took care of him today."

Their son-in-law, Mason, had taken the boys to his shop where he repairs four-wheel-drive vehicles. Around ten in the morning a piece of equipment used to lift cars dropped on three-year-old Keith's hand.

When Mason heard Keith scream and saw what had happened, fear gripped him. He felt certain he would find Keith's fingers crushed or even cut off. When he freed Keith's little hand, he found one small cut on a finger. The entire family praised God for Keith's protection.

Learning Problems

When we pray for specific problems, sometimes the answers come quickly. When our vivacious daughter, Kimberly, entered tenth grade, she floundered academically. I found the promise in Isaiah 54:13 a great encouragement so I personalized it into a prayer for her. *"All thy children* (including Kimberly) *shall be taught of the Lord; and great shall be the peace of thy children* (KJV).

After praying we visited her counselor. She advised a different level of classes, a self-paced math class, and an opportunity to be a teacher's helper. Kim received nothing less than B grades the next grading period. God, who helped us pray, also answered our prayers.

Speech Therapy

Sometimes specific prayers can take a very long time to be answered. Larry, our oldest son, had speech problems from the time he first learned to talk. We knew this fit into God's healing realm because of Jesus' demonstration when He was confronted with a deaf man who could hardly talk. Jesus took the man aside and healed his deafness, then *his tongue was loosened and he began to speak plainly* (Mark 7:35).

We decided to trust God in this matter. Though Larry received no instant healing, we watched God provide in unusual ways. After a difficult first grade in Johnstown, Pennsylvania, Larry was involved in the choice to repeat that grade. (That decision placed him in the same grade with his younger brother, David, throughout his school years.) It was school policy to provide no speech therapy until the second grade. They made an exception. Larry was the only first grader in speech therapy that year.

We lived in Eugene, Oregon, when Larry attended sixth grade. I asked my Bible study group to pray about Larry's speech problems. Once, after a night of fitful sleep, I awakened with a resolve to contact the junior high school and aggressively pursue speech therapy for Larry. I had been previously told none was available. I made two calls to Larry's advisor, but he wasn't in his office. Two days later, Larry asked, "Mom, did you talk to Mr. Early about speech therapy for me?"

His question surprised me. "No. Why?"

"I talked with two speech therapists today, and I'm going to be meeting regularly with one of them."

I prayed silently, *Lord, forgive me for trying to make things happen instead of trusting You.*

In his middle-school years we moved to Clifton Park, New York. Once again, God made an exception for Larry. The ninth grade had no speech therapist available, but soon Larry was being transported by a special school van to a school-sponsored therapist.

Now a college graduate, Larry still has a slight remnant of his speech problems. He learned to substitute words he can handle for difficult ones. New acquaintances think he has a slight foreign accent. We would have preferred an instant healing, but God used Larry's special needs to build our faith in His provision. We always remember God's ways are higher than ours.

UNDERCOVER CHRISTIAN

It's rewarding to look back at the spiritual growth within my family. I keep a folder of papers from David's second grade work because one of them is a tribute to being raised in a home with God-honoring priorities—like Sunday school every week. It was Christmas so David wrote, "Christmas is God's birthday. And if you don't believe it, just ask my mother."

This was evidence to Darrel and me of another of our covering prayers based on a Bible promise: *And I will pour out My Spirit and My blessings on your children. They shall thrive like watered grass, like willows on a riverbank. "I am the Lord's," they'll proudly say...*(Isaiah 44:3-5, TLB).

All three of our children invited Jesus to be their Lord and Savior during the years we attended Coburg Christian Church on the outskirts of Eugene, Oregon. David and Larry both received the baptism of the Holy Spirit in their early teens. Although Larry and Kim each have a special story, I'll share David's.

It was difficult to talk with David about spiritual matters during high school years. He was very involved in sports, had lots of friends, and tried to talk us out of making him go to church each week—to no avail. However, he invited two friends to accompany him and Larry on a week-long outing with Campus Life in Ocean City, New Jersey. While snapshots proved they had a wild time, his friend Eric confided to me, "I got religion last week, Mrs. Gordon."

When David graduated from Shenendehowa High School in Clifton Park, New York, he received a trophy called the "Body, Mind, and Spirit Award." The recipient is voted by teammates as the person they'd miss most if he weren't on the team. I secretly believed it was for *my* encouragement—God letting me know David was walking in the Spirit.

A cadet at the U. S. Air Force Academy in Colorado Springs, Colorado, Dave managed to keep so busy he went to church infrequently. Parachuting captured his interest and he became part of the Wings of Blue Parachute Team. All of his Sundays were spent in that pursuit. How I grieved and prayed for his spiritual welfare.

Eventually he attended a Bible study held in the room of an upperclassman. At the beginning of Dave's third year God chose a new roommate for him. They were already good friends and shared an enthusiastic interest in weight lifting. Kevin came from a Catholic home.

"We often have discussions about Christian stuff, and we agreed we have to find the answers in the Bible or they don't stand up," Dave told me. "I'd like a good study Bible for Christmas."

He didn't have to wait until Christmas. I immediately searched the nearest Christian bookstore and selected *The Open Bible* because of its extensive reference material. I mailed it promptly.

These two young men had left home with the faith of their parents. Now God was working out the individual faith of each. In their senior year, Dave and Kevin had a weekly Bible study group meeting in *their* room. Each cadet was to take a turn leading the study. If he didn't follow through, Dave always had something prepared.

After graduation David became engaged to a former classmate. They decided their life priorities included God first, and each other second.

I offer this story to encourage you to trust that God is at work answering your prayers for you children—even when the evidence is missing.

HUSBANDS AND WIVES

Few marriage partners are at the same place spiritually. Unless you're reading this book with your spouse, my guess is you've prayed often for his or her spiritual hunger to increase. Have patience. God hears those prayers. *For the unbelieving husband has been sanctified through his wife, and the unbelieving wife has been sanctified through her believing husband. Otherwise your children would be unclean, but as it is, they are holy* (1 Corinthians 7:14).

Sometimes we must wait what seems like forever before we see the results of our prayers. Crissy prayed for ten years through good times and stormy ones for her husband to know Jesus as his Lord. She knew he had come a long way from unbelief when he started giving her prayer requests. Finally, in the middle of a job transfer while he spent time in his new location without his family, Crissy responded to his latest request differently. "I think God would like to do business with you directly."

He knew she spoke the truth. Shortly after that conversation he gave his heart to the Lord.

Robyn had a different experience. Before her husband knew Jesus, she often woke in the middle of the night with a burden on her heart for him. Her special times of prayer occasionally lasted two or three hours. She'd return to bed and wake up in the morning feeling refreshed. Her husband invited Jesus to be his Lord and Savior within three months of her nighttime prayer vigils.

HOSTILE TERRITORY

Often the workplace feels like hostile territory with its unique pressures, problems and personalities. Darrel and I begin our day praying together for the needs ahead. We have some favorite scriptures for just such a place.

- *For surely, O Lord, You bless the righteous; You surround them with your favor as with a shield* (Psalm 5:12).
- *"No weapon forged against you will prevail, and you will refute every tongue that accuses you. This is the heritage of the servants of the Lord, and this is their vindication from me,"* declares the Lord (Isaiah 54:17).
- *For promotion and power come from nowhere on earth, but only from God. He promotes one and deposes another* (Psalm 75:6-7 TLB).

MORE PRAYER PATTERNS

I have a larger collection of Scripture patterns in this segment of my personal manual than I have in any of the others. We are most familiar with the needs of our family members, and we are more involved in their successes and difficulties. These examples will add power to your family prayers:

- *The seed of the righteous shall be delivered* (Proverbs 11:21b KJV).
- *May your strength match the length of your days. There is none like the God of Jerusalem—He descends from the heavens in majestic splendor to help you* (Deuteronomy 33:25b-26 TLB).
- *They will still bear fruit in old age, they will stay fresh and green...*(Psalm 92:14).
- *The Lord Himself is my inheritance, my prize. He is my food and drink, my highest joy! He guards all that is mine* (Psalm 16:5 TLB).
- *See, I have chosen Bezalel... and I have filled him with the Spirit of God, with skill, ability and knowledge in all kinds of crafts...and to engage in all kinds of craftsmanship* (Exodus 31:2-5).
- *And give unto Solomon my son a perfect heart, to keep thy commandments, thy testimonies, and thy statutes...*(1 Chronicles 29:19 KJV).

YOUR PERSONAL PRAYER MANUAL

Label the sixth divider in your prayer manual "My Family." The scriptures you collect here will firmly establish your heart in the knowledge that God cares for families. By now you have discovered the confidence that comes when your prayers grow in the fertile soil of God's Word.

This segment will be more workable if one page is devoted to each family member. Initially, you may wish to add only one new person each day. An important exercise is to list all the qualities you are thankful for in each family member. This prevents the pages from becoming just a want list, and it sows gratitude in our hearts. At first it looks like a lot of white space, but with passing weeks each page will become a progress log with many dates of answered prayers.

When you return to these pages later, the Holy Spirit may lead you to thank God for His intervention in these matters, even though the answer is not yet evident. Mark 11:24 encourages this kind of response: *Therefore I tell you, whatever you ask for in prayer, believe that you have received it, and it will be yours.*

EXAMINE YOURSELF

1. Am I willing to acknowledge that each member of my family belongs primarily to God?
2. Have I asked God to help me see my family as He sees them?
3. Have I asked God to purify my love for each one—to exchange my selfish, judgmental, smothering love for His love?
4. What do I need to relinquish in order that God's best plan for each family member is the thrust of my prayers?
5. Am I willing to wait for God's timing before I see the answers to some of my prayers?

Beloved Father God, thank You for the assurance that You love my family members even more than I do. Help me desire what You desire for them. Lead me to pray heaven's best blessings for them as they blossom under Your loving guidance. Holy Spirit, direct my daily thoughts and prayers for them. Block any prayers that may hinder Your best plan for their lives. Keep eternity in my prayers and in their lives. In the precious name of Jesus Christ I pray. Amen.

"God has established certain irrevocable principles in the universe. He will move in the affairs of mankind according to the degree and how specifically we pray. This is why God is looking for a man to intercede…. God has all power. He has the love and is fully willing to bring change in the world. But He stands astonished, even shocked, when we don't pray. God is crying out to His people: 'I want to move. I want to bless. I want to save. I want to protect, provide, and stop injustice. Why won't you intercede?'"[1]

—Dean Sherman

CHAPTER EIGHT

Into the Harvest Fields

There's no doubt about Jesus' mission. He said, *For the Son of Man came to seek and to save what was lost* (Luke 19:10). He delegated this responsibility to believers in one of His last recorded conversations. *Therefore go and make disciples of all nations…*(Matthew 28:19).

You'd think lost souls, people who don't know about God's great love, would be the number one concern for every Christian. Wrong. According to reports only about six percent of those who call themselves Christian ever lead someone to a personal relationship with Christ.

GOD'S VISION

Before we get further into the subject of praying for the lost, we need to discover why those who are actively involved in winning others to Christ are an endangered species—a little less rare than a California condor. We must begin by praying for ourselves, that our hearts might break with the things that grieve the heart of God.

We see pictures of emaciated children with the bloated stomachs from starvation and we are touched with compassion. God sees these physical needs and more. He looks on the inside of every person while we merely see the outside. He can look inside well-fed, well-clothed people surrounded with the wealth of the world and grieve, because He sees emaciated, starving spirits inside.

The part He sees has eternal value. Our prayers need to include a request that God will help us see the unsaved as He sees them and that He will give us a zeal to share the good news of God's love.

ONE BY ONE

Our focus needs to be on praying for the unsaved as individuals. This chapter logically follows the one on praying for our family. It's an uncommon family that doesn't have some members whose names are not yet written in the Lamb's Book of Life in heaven. As family members our concern and pain approaches God's anguish. We are encouraged knowing He is not willing that any should be lost. We are less patient waiting for the answers to our prayers for our family members because we care so much more than for the unnamed masses.

Remember the two husbands mentioned in the previous chapter? I related the salvation experiences there because that's the chapter in the prayer manual where a separate page is given to each family member. Prayers for an unsaved spouse will draw power and encouragement from this chapter, too.

WAITING PRAYERS

We can take courage from the prayer journals of George Muller. "God, he estimated, had answered over 50,000 of his prayers, many thousand of which were answered on the day he made them and often before he arose from his knees. Some of his petitions, however, lingered across the decades. Here is a sample of such asking...

"In November 1844, I began to pray for the conversion of five individuals. I prayed everyday without a single intermission, whether sick or in health, on the land or on the sea, and whatever the pressure of my engagements might be. Eighteen months elapsed before the first of the five was converted."[1]

Five years passed before the second, and another six before the third was converted. After thirty-six years the last two remained unconverted. "But I hope in God, I pray on, and look yet for the answer. They are not converted yet, but they will be."[2]

At the time of Muller's death in 1898 he had prayed daily for fifty-two years for these two men, sons of a friend from his youth. He left a legacy of prayer, for after Mr. Muller's death God brought them into His fold.

His record makes my waiting in prayer look puny by comparison. I am encouraged by Muller's faith in God to answer his prayers.

THE GREAT EXCHANGE

In a time of prayer when I had great concern for a neighbor and wasn't sure how to pray, a simple prayer formed in my heart. "Lord, exchange Your light for her darkness, and Your truth for her error. Exchange a new heart for her heart of stone."

I began using this prayer frequently, but I thought it was much too simple to be a very good prayer. However, in my Bible reading, I found many confirmations that this was a powerful scriptural prayer.

Another prayer I often speak is, "Holy Spirit, bless him with the gift of conviction." We don't normally think of conviction as a gift, but if it leads a person to receive Jesus as Lord, nothing could be greater.

When I'm driving along and see someone I sense needs prayer, I offer, "Lord, have mercy on that person. May Your Kingdom come and Your will be done in his/her life." Unless the Holy Spirit prompts me differently, that's the end of the prayer. I often wonder if I may have said the only prayer for that person in ages.

It isn't hard to come up with a list of people who don't know the joy and peace of having Jesus as their Lord and Savior. However it's possible God desires a willingness in our hearts to be the answer to our prayers. God uses people, not angels, to proclaim His Word to the lost.

Our lives are our testimony. St. Francis of Assisi said, "Preach the gospel at all times—if necessary use words."

CHRISTMAS OPPORTUNITY

Almost fifty years ago, long before it became almost universal, I carefully composed a Christmas letter to friends and family who lived far away. I've done it annually since then because we have so many long-distance friends. It always contains scripture and a tribute to the love of Christ evident in our lives. I include the tears and triumphs of the previous year—with a one-page limit. I pray over it hoping it will draw others to Jesus.

After 25 years I received a wonderful letter from a 75-year-old uncle telling me he'd found a new relationship with Jesus. I wondered if I'd been the only one praying for him.

BE PREPARED

During the time we lived in Clifton Park, New York, I volunteered as an ambulance attendant. When my portable alarm wailed, I grabbed coat and keys and drove to the ambulance garage. I always prayed, "Lord, I wouldn't be making this trip if You weren't with me. Help the person I'm called to aid, and help me give physical and spiritual support."

I vividly remember one transportation call. We arrived at the home of a man critically ill from the ravages of cancer. His room reeked from the offensive smell of the bandages over his draining wounds. We took him by stretcher to the ambulance. My co-workers happily rode in the front seats on the trip to the hospital, leaving me alone with the distraught, anxious 50-year-old father and the stench.

God enabled me to tenderly share Jesus' love and promises during our trip together. We had a beautiful time of prayer before we arrived at the hospital. I left him with a small blue New Testament, the one I usually kept in my coat pocket in case God gave me opportunities like this.

The other attendants proclaimed me a hero. "How could you stand the smell?"

I was too busy doing God's business to notice.

GOD'S PAINT BRUSHES

I was part owner of an artists' co-op art gallery in Eugene, Oregon, and quite involved in art shows of my paintings when I sensed my priorities were out of balance. In prayer, I physically handed my crock of brushes to God. "I won't paint again, Lord, until it's clear You give me permission."

Shortly after, I was asked to teach painting for the community college. The class would be at the nearby elementary school and the pay was tempting. I prayed about it. "God, if you don't want me doing this, then let there be so little interest the minimum enrollment of twelve students won't be met."

The first night thirteen came. Before every class I prayed for the students. God provided many opportunities to minister to spiritual needs while I taught oils, acrylics and watercolor painting to men and women with beginning and intermediate skills.

"The doctor says I need to take it easy. That's great for him to say. Just how am I supposed to do that?" My student Penny asked. She and I met after class and I told her about Jesus, Who was waiting to take her burdens and bring the peace and healing she needed.

When God gave me permission to use my brushes again, I realized they provided unique opportunities to tell of His loving care for those who trust Him.

CONVERSATION STARTERS

God brings unusual openings to tell others about Him when I'm willing and prepared to participate. Our fifteen-year-old house in suburban Seattle needed many improvements to weatherize it against heat loss on cold, wintry days. A series of service people visited our home over several weeks.

Two men emerged from the dark crawl space under the house where they had insulated the sub-flooring. When they declared their task finished, I handed each a small blue New Testament. "When life gets dark and closes in on you like that crawl space, the love letters in here will lead you to the One who will bring His light into your life."

Three men replaced our single-paned windows with double panes. After I inspected their work, I gave each a New Testament. "When the storms of life threaten you, here's a book that will help you through them even better than double-paned windows. I know the Author. He loves you and has a wonderful plan for your life."

The carpet layer surveyed his well-stretched beige masterpiece and pronounced, "May it last forever."

"It probably won't," I said, "but let me share something with you that will…" He left with a New Testament in his pocket.

A car driven by a teen-age boy careened out of control and broke off our mailbox post at the ground. Scared but unhurt, he and a friend soon returned to replace the damaged post.

"If you drive like that often, you're going to need help. You need to know how to keep angels watching over you…" I extended a pale blue New Testament to each smiling teen.

PLAYING HOUSE

I previously told how Corrie ten Boom became an intercessor at age five. The complete incident is a fine illustration of staying alert to moments the Holy Spirit provides.

"One day my mother was watching me play house. In my little girl world of fantasy, she saw that I was pretending to call on a neighbor. I knocked on the make-believe door and waited…no one answered.

" 'Corrie, I know Someone who is standing at your door and knocking right now.'

"Was she playing a game with me? I know now that there was a preparation within my childish heart for that moment; the Holy Spirit makes us ready for acceptance of Jesus Christ, of turning our life over to Him.

" 'Jesus said that He is standing at the door, and if you invite Him in He will come into your heart,' my mother continued. 'Would you like to invite Jesus in?'

"At that moment my mother was the most beautiful person in the whole world to me.

" 'Yes, Mama, I want Jesus in my heart.'

"So she took my little hand in hers and we prayed together."[3]

COMA

Ted's 16-year-old son, Philip, had been in an auto accident. In critical condition, he was in the intensive care unit connected to a cardiac monitor. The doctor held out little hope for the boy's survival. Ted invited two friends he considered prayer warriors to accompany him into Philip's room. The father feared his son had never received Jesus. The little group spoke to Philip as if he could hear them, though in his comatose condition he gave no indication this was so.

They noticed visible changes on the cardiac monitor each time they spoke of Jesus. Encouraged, they told Philip about Jesus' provision of paying the penalty for our sins with His death on the cross and His promise of heaven. When Ted asked if Philip wanted to accept Jesus, again the monitor registered significant change. The three felt there had been communication with Philip though he was not able to respond with words. They prayed with him.

Philip's earthly life ceased shortly after this experience. Ted is comforted by a peace God gave him at that time. He treasures the memory of those moments when Philip's spirit responded although his body couldn't. He is grateful for the godly friends who were sensitive and alert not to miss an important moment.

PATTERNS AND PROMISES

We can be certain we are praying in God's perfect will when we pray for others to meet Jesus as their Savior and Lord. The following scriptures will help direct those prayers.

- *But do not forget this one thing, dear friends: With the Lord a day is like a thousand years, and a thousand years are like a day. The Lord is not slow in keeping His promise, as some understand slowness. He is patient with you, not wanting anyone to perish, but everyone to come to repentance* (2 Peter 3:8).
- *Here I am! I stand at the door and knock. If anyone hears My voice and opens the door, I will go in and eat with him, and he with Me"* (Revelation 3:20).
- *For God so loved the world that He gave His one and only Son, that whoever believes in Him shall not perish but have eternal life. For God did not send His Son into the world to condemn the world, but to save the world through Him. Whoever believes in Him is not condemned, but whoever does not believe stands condemned already because he has not believed in the name of God's one and only Son"* (John 3:16-18).
- *If you confess with your mouth, "Jesus is Lord," and believe in your heart that God raised Him from the dead, you will be saved* (Romans 10:9).
- *For it is by grace you have been saved, through faith—and this not from yourselves, it is the gift of God—not by works so that no one can boast* (Ephesians 2:8).
- *So get rid of all that is wrong in your life, both inside and outside, and humbly be glad for the wonderful message we have received, for it is able to save our souls as it takes hold of your hearts* (James 1:21 TLB).
- *Therefore, if anyone is in Christ, he is a new creation; the old has gone, the new has come* (2Corinthians 5:17)!

YOUR PERSONAL PRAYER MANUAL

Title this divider in your prayer manual, "The Unsaved." God has already filled you with compassion for many who are yet to become joint heirs with Jesus Christ. Begin a list of those in your family, your friends, neighbors, and co-workers who don't know Jesus. Date each entry and leave room for a date on which the answer to your prayers becomes evident. Remember, *There is rejoic-*

ing in the presence of the angels of God over one sinner who repents (Luke 15:10).

The scripture promises above are a good beginning for your collection. When your Bible reading reveals examples of God's mercy toward sinners, add them here.

Ask the Holy Spirit to help you with your list. He may lead you to pray for the entire list as a whole, or He may direct you to pray for an individual in a fresh, new way.

EXAMINE YOURSELF

1. Have I been blind to the needs of my neighbors? My co-workers?
2. In reading this chapter, what is something I've been convicted about?
3. The love of God flows through me to others (check one): slightly_____, moderately_____, needs improvement _____, so much that I often weep for lost souls_____.
4. Am I willing to be known as a Christian and speak up when the opportunity seems right?
5. Is my lifestyle different enough from that of unbelievers to be a testimony even if I used no words?

Beloved Holy Spirit, I desire to be a partner with you in the salvation of those within the circle of my life. Help me see what God sees in them. Fill my heart with a godly compassion to pray more earnestly, and to be about the business of loving others into the Kingdom of God. Help me pray for all of these whose names are not yet written in the Lamb's Book of Life. I pray in the precious name of my Lord, Jesus. Amen.

"Faith is the prime essential when it comes to appropriating God's gifts. It is not surprising, therefore, that the adversary would seek to undermine our faith by diverting our attention from the "faithfulness and worthiness" of the Giver to questions concerning the validity of the gift."[4]

—Dr. Robert C. Frost

CHAPTER NINE

Equipped to Harvest

WHERE IS THE POWER?

Some Christians are powerless in their daily walk while others have a power source that permeates all their activities. It's not God's will that we be powerless, but many who profess belief in Jesus seem unaware of this. Before Jesus ascended, He told His faithful followers, "*You will receive power when the Holy Spirit comes upon you; and you will be My witnesses…*(Acts 2:4)." This first encounter with new power came to 120 people as they were filled with the Holy Spirit on the day of Pentecost.

The gift of the Holy Spirit is intended for all believers. To those 3000 who listened to Peter's Pentecost sermon and desired to enter God's kingdom, Peter said, "*Repent and be baptized, every one of you, in the name of Jesus Christ so that your sins may be forgiven. And you will receive the gift of the Holy Spirit. The promise is for you and your children and for all who are far off—for all whom the Lord our God will call*" (Acts 2:38-39).

The apostle Paul speaks of those "*having the form of religion but denying its power*" (2 Timothy 3:5). Some remain powerless because we have the right to receive or reject the help and fellowship of the Holy Spirit. Scripture tells us not to quench or grieve the Holy

Spirit. We are called to be continually filled with the Holy Spirit, to walk in the Spirit, and to be aglow with the Spirit.

THE DEEPER EXPERIENCE

James Gilchrist Lawson, in his book *Deeper Experiences of Famous Christians,* written in 1911, examined biographies and journals of Christians across the centuries who were pre-eminent because of their piety and spiritual power. Lawson spent years in the greatest libraries of Europe and America searching Christian literature of all ages. His object was to describe *in their own words* the deepest spiritual experiences of the most famous Christians.

"When Christians of so many different centuries and countries relate their deeper Christian experiences in their own manner and language, and yet all agree to the essential facts, it is overwhelming evidence in favor of the fact that such a deep Christian experience may really be attained."[1]

"The persons described relate their deeper experiences in very different terms; but the deeper Christian experience is always the same. It is the baptism, or filling, or gift of the Holy Spirit, and the experience resulting from being 'filled with the Spirit.' The Methodist may describe this experience as 'entire sanctification,' 'holiness,' or 'perfect love.' The Baptist may call it the 'filling of the Spirit.' The Presbyterian may call it the 'life of faith,' or 'rest of faith,' or the 'full assurance of faith.' The Congregationalist may call it 'entire consecration.' The Quaker may call it 'living in the Spirit,' or 'walking in the Spirit,' or 'over-coming power.' The old Roman Catholic and Greek Church writers may term it 'death to the self-life,' or 'pure love.' All these are Scriptural terms, or ideas, and all refer to a Spirit-filled Christian experience."[2]

I value Lawson's century-old book. He quoted many historical men and women in addition to those in the Old and New Testaments. He offers moving proof of the unity of God's purpose throughout time. Volumes could be added if we were to include Spirit-filled twentieth century Christians.

POWER FOR BELIEVERS

One contemporary example of the power of the baptism with the Holy Spirit is in the ministry of Teen Challenge. The organization was founded by David Wilkerson, whose story is told in *The Cross and The Switchblade*.[3] Teen Challenge brings addicts, drug peddlers, gang members, and prostitutes into a personal relationship with Jesus Christ and the baptism with the Holy Spirit. They commonly see life-changing results. Deliverance from drug addiction and destructive lifestyles is part of Teen Challenge's unprecedented success. Secular drug rehabilitation programs have never achieved a comparable success rate.

According to Wilkerson, it takes more than a love for Jesus and a compassion for lost souls to qualify us as His witnesses. "You must realize you do not have all Jesus wants you to have unless you are baptized with the Holy Ghost."[4]

I ENTER IN

My heart has always been tender and open to God. I credit my praying grandmother for that. At age 12 I responded to an altar call and experienced water baptism in the First Baptist Church in Bakersfield, California. Neither my mother nor father had any obvious relationship with God. Through subsequent years, I was the recipient of God's protection and I grew in my knowledge of the Lord.

When I was 40 years old, a friend mailed me several books that introduced me to the Baptism with the Holy Spirit: Don Basham's *Face Up With a Miracle*; Pat Boone's *A New Song*; John Sherrill's *They Speak With Other Tongues*; Dr. Robert Frost's *Aglow With the Spirit*; Dr. John Rea's *Layman's commentary on the Holy Spirit*.

Each of these sent me searching the New Testament to verify what I had read. I soon prayed to receive the baptism with the Holy Spirit. "Lord, I desire to walk in the fullness of all you intend for me. I ask you, according to the promises in Your Word, to baptize me with your Holy Spirit."

In the days and weeks following my prayer I moved into a new realm. I experienced a great hunger to read the Bible. The Word contained a vitality I had never experienced. From the freshness of personal revelations, I felt as if the ink might still be wet. My eyes were opened to see new things in the Bible. My ears were opened to hear the Holy Spirit speaking within, guiding, directing, and comforting. My knowledge of Jesus was transformed into a sweet, wonderful fellowship. My times of prayer were alive with a new relationship with the living God—Father, Son, and Holy Spirit.

After two weeks, I wondered why I had not yet received the gift of a prayer language—speaking in tongues. Dr. Frost's words in *Aglow With the Spirit* encouraged me. He pointed out, as our personal salvation is a free gift of God's grace, unearned by our work, so it is with the baptism with the Holy Spirit. If you've asked, you have received. I needed that affirmation. I prayed, "Lord, I don't want to restrict Your gifts. If You want me to have a special prayer language, then I am willing and eager to receive."

As I yielded my voice, the first sounds embarrassed me—rather like baby talk. When I persisted, the flow of sounds became rhythmical and almost melodious. Surely these words were a perfect prayer, for we are told, *"We do not know what we ought to pray, but the Spirit himself intercedes for us with groans that words cannot express...in accordance with God's will* (Romans 8:26-27).

During the 28 years between ages 12 and 40, I had God's peace, protection and direction but my Promised Land experience is exhilarating compared with my wilderness trek. I encourage new believers to receive the baptism with the Holy Spirit without delay. That was the experience of the early church.

APPOINTMENT

To follow up on Darrel's heart health after his hospitalization in Milwaukee with a heart attack, I made an appointment with a cardiologist in nearby Eugene, Oregon. A busy specialist, he had no available openings for four weeks. The date was on our calendar, but Darrel's health was so good we forgot about it.

The day of the appointment Darrel took his father and two sons and went duck hunting. I was shocked when I saw Darrel's three o'clock appointment on the calendar. He needed to be home by 1:30 pm in order to clean up, change clothes and get to the doctor's office on time. I told Darrel's mother the details. "I'm going to pray that God will somehow have him home by 1:30 so we can keep this appointment."

She only smiled, but I suspect she thought I was weird.

At one o'clock I went upstairs to get ready to go with him. When I glanced out the window I saw Darrel's car drive into the yard. "Thank You, God!" I rejoiced.

"We got rained out," he replied. He kept his appointment.

The cardiologist announced, "I find no evidence of any previous heart attack."

We praised God all the way home.

This episode began with my prayer of faith. It served as a powerful example to Darrel, his parents, and me on how God will answer bold, believing prayers. I expected God's intervention and acted on it before I saw any evidence of an answer. The Holy Spirit motivated my faith and boldness.

FRUITFUL

My sons' 6th grade Sunday school teacher told me they had been studying the fruit of the Spirit as listed in Galatians 5: *But when the Holy Spirit controls our lives He will produce this kind of fruit in us: love, joy, peace, patience, kindness, goodness, faithfulness, gentleness and self control…*(TLB). She asked the boys to think of someone they knew who was living an example of the fruit of the Spirit.

She told me, "Marge, you need to know one of your sons raised his hand and said, 'my mother.'"

Her words were a special treasure to me. Before I received the baptism with the Holy Spirit, my tongue needed beauty treatments. Besides using a few offensive four-letter words, I would yell at my children when I was impatient or angry with them. What a relief to know the Holy Spirit had been replacing my bad habits with the fruit of the Spirit. I've discovered life isn't a do-it-yourself project when you are walking in the Spirit.

Patterns and Promises

- *John answered them all, "I baptize you with water. But one more powerful than I will come, the thongs of whose sandals I am not worthy to untie. He will baptize you with the Holy Spirit and with fire (Luke 3:16)."*

- *If you love Me, you will obey what I command. And I will ask the Father, and He will give you another Counselor to be with you forever—the Spirit of truth. The world cannot accept Him, because it neither sees Him nor knows Him. But you know Him, for He lives with you and will be in you (John 14:15-17).*

- *If you, though you are evil, know how to give good gifts to your children, how much more will your Father in heaven give the Holy Spirit to those who ask Him (Luke 11:13)!*

- *Does God give you His Spirit and work miracles among you because you observe the law, or because you believe what you heard (Galatians 3:5)?*

- *Christ redeemed us from the curse of the law…He redeemed us in order that the blessing given to Abraham might come to the Gentiles through Christ Jesus, so that by faith we might receive the promise of the Spirit (Galatians 3:13-14).*

- *When Paul placed his hands on them, the Holy Spirit came on them, and they spoke in tongues and prophesied (Acts 19:6).*

- *For anyone who speaks in a tongue does not speak to men but to God. Indeed, no one understands him; he utters mysteries with his spirit (I Corinthians 14:2).*

- *Now it is God who makes both us and you stand firm in Christ. He anointed us, set His seal of ownership on us, and put His Spirit in our hearts as a deposit, guaranteeing what is to come (2 Corinthians 1:21-22).*

- *We have not received the spirit of the world but the Spirit who is from God, that we may understand what God has freely given us (1 Corinthians 2:12).*

Personal Prayer Manual

The next divider can be labeled "Power." Ask the Holy Spirit to direct you as you add names of believers needing His power in their lives. Remember to leave a space to date the answer to your prayers.

Our God is a God of miracles. He rejoices when we are obedient to His will. Holy Spirit baptism is a miracle and is only a beginning. Walking in the Spirit means saying, "Lord, I can't do it, but You can." If the answers to your prayers are slow in coming, don't be discouraged. Remember, *with God, all things are possible* (Matthew 19:26).

Examine Yourself

- Am I only a professing Christian or a possessing Christian, walking in the fullness of all God has for prepared for me?
- Do I have the form of religion and none of its power?
- Am I willing to receive everything Jesus wants for me?
- Have I hesitated to share the Holy Spirit Baptism with other believers?

Dear Jesus, cleanse me from all unrighteousness and baptize me with your Spirit. Thank you, Heavenly Father, for the incomparable gift of your Holy Spirit as my personal advocate, counselor and friend. Dear Holy Spirit, forgive me when I have grieved you. Fill me continually. Forgive me for neglecting to use the powerful gift of praying in tongues, speaking to God. Remind me daily to walk in Your power, not mine. Give me boldness and sensitivity as I have opportunity to share Jesus with others. Help me introduce others to You and Your gifts. In Jesus' wonderful name. Amen

"Heaven's storehouse is not a center that periodically is in short supply and which we must guard by being careful to ask with appropriate reserve. God isn't rationing answers to prayer as though there was a shortage on His ability to beget, provide, heal or produce."[5]

—Jack Hayford

CHAPTER TEN

Workers in the Harvest

DELEGATED AUTHORITY

In unfolding the mystery of His plan, God made it plain all believers are part of one another and important to each other. He has made us all fishers of men, sowers of seed, and ministers of His good news. *So in Christ we who are many form one body, and each member belongs to all the others* (Romans 12:5).

Our gifts differ and ministries vary, but the goal is the same. We are all involved in telling others that God loves them and has a wonderful plan for their lives. When one is weak, we are all weakened. When one is suffering, all suffer. When one is triumphant, we all share in that victory.

We are best acquainted with workers for the harvest of souls in our local church: the members, pastors, elders, deacons, teachers, and others in ministry. Someone once observed that the shepherd doesn't make new sheep—sheep make new sheep.

The extended church includes missionary activities and organizations within denominations and nondenominational ministries like the Gideons International. Some are involved in refugee resettlement, the care of orphans, Christian television and radio. The suffering Church in third-world countries is an important part of the Body of Christ.

Think of these and others as you study the following passages.

Patterns and Promises

- *He told them, "The harvest is plentiful, but the workers are few. Ask the Lord of the harvest, therefore, to send out workers into His harvest field"* (Luke 10:2).
- *Finally, brothers, pray for us that the message of the Lord may spread rapidly and be honored, just as it was with you. And pray that we may be delivered from wicked and evil men, for not everyone has faith* (2 Thessalonians 3:1-2).
- *So is My Word that goes out from My mouth: It will not return to Me empty, but will accomplish what I desire and achieve the purpose for which I sent it* (Isaiah 55:11).
- *May our Lord Jesus Christ Himself and God our Father, who loved us and by His grace gave us eternal encouragement and good hope, encourage your hearts and strengthen you in every good deed and word* (2 Thessalonians 2:16-17).
- *Now He who supplies seed to the sower and bread for food will also supply and increase your store of seed and will enlarge the harvest of your righteousness* (2 Corinthians 9:10).
- *Devote yourselves to prayer, being watchful and thankful. And pray for us, too, that God may open a door for our message, so that we may proclaim the mystery of Christ, for which I am in chains. Pray that I may proclaim it clearly, as I should* (Colossians 4:2-4).
- *And pray in the Spirit on all occasions with all kinds of prayers and requests. With this in mind, be alert and always keep on praying for all the saints. Pray also for me, that whenever I open my mouth, words may be given me so that I will fearlessly make known the mystery of the Gospel...* (Ephesians 6:18-19).

Prayer Support

Whenever Christian workers request support, it always includes a call for prayer. Prayer releases power in many ways: Doors of opportunity are opened. The path is made clear. Healing comes. Discouragement and fear are lifted. Enemies are defeated. Many people are added to the Kingdom of God.

FAVOR IN VIENNA

Wayde Goodall, former pastor of Calvary Temple (now Northwest Family Church) in Auburn, Washington, tells of God's incredible answer to prayer in Vienna in the mid 1980s. "God sent a family to start a church in a country where they could not speak the language, did not know the people and did not know the 'how to'. We had no other option but to trust the Lord to open doors and give us favor in the city. We prayed for just that."

They arrived in Vienna on Thursday, and started the church the following Sunday with about 20 people. In six weeks over 90 people attended. At the end of a year, Vienna Christian Center was one of the largest churches in Austria.

THE JESUS FILM PROJECT

An amazing tool to reach those who have never heard of Jesus is the JESUS film. It is entirely based on the Word of God. Understood in the local language of the people, it is currently available in 933 tongues. The project's goal is that JESUS will someday be available to reach every tribe, nation, people and tongue.

The JESUS Film Project has partnered with other mission organizations and churches to see many millions of people make decisions for Christ. Prayers are an important part of the JESUS Film Project to provide equipment, films, and training for workers and volunteers. Amazingly, 2,419 traveling film teams are at work in 106 countries as well as hundreds of partnership teams with other organizations.[1] Our prayers can help protect them from the enemies of Christ during times of great danger.

Amazing reports come from these teams. A film team traveled in a remote area of central Asia, where many hazards await Christians. Lost, they stopped to get their bearings.

A man approached, waving excitedly. "You are they! You are they! You are the men in my dream! Can you tell me the truth?" He had a dream in which he saw men coming to him. A voice said they would bring him Truth.

The JESUS team invited him into their car and he directed them to his village over dirt roads. That evening the team showed JESUS to the men of the community gathered in the man's teahouse, and again in his home. He and his whole household became followers of Christ.

A team in Africa had gone halfway up a mountain to show the film. They set up the equipment and spread the word about the film showing. Despite their hard work and prayer, the crowd was small and only a few people decided to follow Christ.

The next morning the team was surprised when nearly a hundred people showed up for follow-up. They wanted prayer for Jesus to forgive their sins, to give them eternal life and be Lord of their lives. These people lived in the valley. They had not seen the film, but the sound from the speakers had reached their village. They were moved by the words they heard.[2]

TELEVISION VICTORIES

Trinity Broadcasting Network declares, "2005 has been without doubt, the greatest year of spiritual harvest in our 32 year history!" Over 12,000 television stations and cable systems worldwide have brought at least two million souls to Christ in 2005. With satellite broadcasts and internet websites, their programming reaches even where missionaries are forbidden. Christian programs are available 24 hours a day. Everyone involved with TBN asserts the importance of prayer in every aspect of its operations.[3]

A viewer in China wrote, "I always watch this channel with computer. And I like your programs. Here I can feel God's love."

A report from Iran: "You blessed me and helped me have a personal relationship with God Almighty through his only Son, our wonderful Lord and Savior Jesus Christ. Because it is impossible for me to attend church here so TBN is church and family for me now...."[4]

PRISON FELLOWSHIP

Prison Fellowship, founded by Charles Colson, is having dramatic results caring for those marginalized by society. New opportunities continue for sharing the Good News of Jesus Christ with captive hearts and minds. They presently anticipate the first women's unit to be added to four pre-existing faith-based prison efforts in Arkansas. Over 500,000 children of prisoners were served at Christmas, 2005, through Prison Fellowship's Angel Tree project.

President Mark Earley writes, "...Your prayers are literally changing lives, and ultimately changing the community, the nation, the world."[5]

BOOK OF HOPE

The Book of Hope is a composite of the four Gospels: Matthew, Mark, Luke and John, with many illustrations appealing to school age children. These were given to 63,000,000 children in 2005, primarily in third world countries. God has amazingly opened doors for school distributions in former communist nations.

In Russia, Victor was hopelessly addicted to drugs, homeless, and considering suicide when he found the *Book of Hope* lying on the ground. He took it back to the place where he was staying with some other addicts and they read it through together. Today, Victor is free from addiction and is serving Jesus. His mother even took him back in.

"Across Western Europe, every major religion except Islam is declining. The drop is most glaring in France, Sweden and the Netherlands, where church attendance is less than 10% in some areas. One reason cited for decline: affluence! People who are assured of a comfortable life have turned their backs on religion. Pray that the Book of Hope, the churches of Europe, and other missions efforts will bring the people of Europe back to a focus on their need for salvation."[6]

Open Doors

Brother Andrew's Open Doors ministry has been supplying Bibles in miraculous ways behind the closed doors of many countries. Their goal for 2006 includes 2,625,500 resource items for the Persecuted Church. The faith of persecuted Christians draws people to Christ. What happened in the early church still happens today. Jailers, torturers, and co-prisoners watch Christians enduring persecution and say, "You have something different—what is it?"

Communism is not the only source of persecution in Southeast Asia. Radical fringe elements from Islam, Hinduism, and Buddhism also oppose Christianity. Yet that oppression is refining and building the Church.

Dr. Carl Moeller, president of Open Doors USA writes, "I plead for your prayers. Our brothers and sisters are in a cauldron of persecution and opposition. They need you to kneel with them, side by side, before God's glorious throne…. I urge you to pray, pray, pray. As you do this you will make a tremendous difference for our suffering brothers and sisters."[7]

Other Ministries

This chapter can't contain all the many ways the Word of God is being made available to those who have never heard of Jesus. A large number of organizations are bringing physical support to those in need in addition to introducing people to Jesus. The Salvation Army and Samaritans Purse are two very effective ministries worldwide.

Campus Crusade for Christ International, founded by Dr. Bill Bright, is distributing Bibles to spiritually hungry people, discipling and training new believers worldwide.

Focus on the Family, founded by Dr. James Dobson, provides radio broadcasts and Christian literature to strengthen families.

Be Specific

Sometimes we need to be reminded to be specific when we pray. A favorite story comes from a report of the Sisterhood of

Mary, the Lutheran sisterhood working to rebuild lives in Germany after World War 2. They were holding children's Bible classes in a small, empty goat stall. Many other needy children waited outside, because only ten at a time fit into the small space. Where could they locate more room?

"One day I took a piece of blue chalk and drew a picture of an old-fashioned bus on the blackboard," Sister Benedikta said. "I told the children, 'Now we are going to pray to the Father in heaven for this bus. And we won't erase the picture until we receive it.'"

A mobile schoolroom would allow the sisters to travel from place to place, visiting and teaching many poor children. Several sisters, children, and their parents joined in praying for the bus. When the drawing was three weeks old, a man came by and asked if they needed a bus. When they went to look at it, they discovered it was bright blue, and an out-dated model like the one drawn on the blackboard. The price exactly matched a sudden inflow of gifts. "God had heard us and given us what we needed."[8]

From this time on, prayer groups began to form, even among the youngest children. They had personally experienced the care of their Father in heaven. God answered their prayers in the specific and literal way children can understand—including a bright blue bus.

PERSONAL PRAYER MANUAL

Label this divider, "Body of Christ." I suggest you insert three empty pages; one each entitled my Local Church, the Extended Church, and the Suffering Church. Your prayers may be different for each. I like to include pictures from newsletters and missionary photos of those I pray for and tape them on these pages. They make my prayers more personal.

Take time to list by name the pastors, teachers, and leaders in your church. You will probably be surprised at the size of your list. Ask each person on your list for a specific prayer request. When we pray specifically, it is easier to identify the answer.

I recall an elderly church member who told me, "I use the church directory and pray through it for everyone in the church at least once a year.

EXAMINE YOURSELF

1. Have I been too nearsighted about the Church, the Body of Christ?
2. What can I do to be better informed about the needs of those who labor in Christ's harvest?

Father God, Jehovah Jireh, You are our provider. For those laboring in Your harvest fields I pray for open doors, boldness in speaking about You, and great fruit for their labors. I pray, too, that You will protect them from the evil one, protect their health, and provide exceeding abundantly for all their needs; physical, financial, and spiritual. Encourage and comfort them. Help me to become better informed about their needs and how to pray for them. I pray in the Name above all names, Jesus Christ. Amen.

"To the degree that intercessors pray, the leaders gain protection against the fiery darts of the wicked one, over and above the whole armor of God they are responsible for using."[9]

—C. Peter Wagner

CHAPTER ELEVEN

The Nation and Those in Authority

GOD IS IN CHARGE

We may not choose or like people who are in authority but we are required to pray for them. *"I urge, then, first of all, that requests, prayers, intercession and thanksgiving be made for everyone—for kings and all those in authority, that we may live peaceful and quiet lives in all godliness and holiness"* (1 Timothy 2:1-2).

The Bible clearly states God is the one who elevates people to positions of power. *"Everyone must submit himself to the governing authorities, for there is no authority except that which God has established. The authorities that exist have been established by God"* (Romans 13:1). Jesus confirms this in His response to Pilate at His trial. *"Jesus answered, 'You would have no power over Me if it were not given to you from above'"* (John 19:11).

When you stand in the gap between God and those in authority, you become a source of blessing and a line of defense for them.

SUPERPOWER

Through Open Doors Ministry, Brother Andrew has provided assistance and Bibles to Christians in countries where Christianity is forbidden. He knows the power of prayer. "Through the keys of the kingdom we have influence in the affairs of the world. We really have more influence than the leaders of the so-called super powers."[1]

God performed remarkable miracles for Open Doors Bible couriers before the Iron Curtain of Russian communism fell. The work continues in Muslim and communist countries as God continues to open doors.

According to examples in God's Word, we have more power through prayer than the combined power of all three branches of our United States government.

ESTHER'S EXAMPLE

The Old Testament book of Esther provides a powerful picture of God's intervention when His people prayed and fasted. A wicked official manipulated King Xerxes into issuing a proclamation to exterminate all Jews on a single day. Queen Esther is encouraged it is her access to the king that may save her people.

Esther made this request: *"Go, gather together all the Jews who are in Susa, and fast for me. Do not eat or drink for three days, night or day. I and my maids will fast as you do. When this is done, I will go to the king, even though it is against the law. And if I perish, I perish"* (Esther 4:15).

Through a series of dramatic events not only are the Jews saved, but also the evil perpetrator, Haman, is hanged on the gallows he prepared for a prominent Jew. The annual Jewish holiday of Purim is a remembrance celebration of God's intervention in answer to the people's prayers.

WORLD WAR 2 VICTORIES

Many well-documented prayers of students and faculty in the Bible College of Wales correlate with Allied victories in World War 2. Using newspaper headlines of the battles and the needs of the Allied troops they were led into deep intercessory prayer. The mighty hand of God stayed a powerful enemy on many fronts. In the book *Rees Howells, Intercessor*, a graphic answer to prayer is recorded about the preparation for the D Day invasion. "I don't think there is anything to compare with the night we invaded Normandy. We said that God was going before our men and it wasn't going to be like Dunkirk. The *Daily Telegraph* reported that it was only that night the U-boats did not patrol the channel. The way we went over to Normandy was beyond imagination—4,000 ships and 11,000 planes—and they never met a single ship or plane of the enemy."[2]

Mr. Howells kept a journal of his prayers and those of the college during those critical times. Many coincide with dramatic changes in the course of the war.

"Mr. Churchill, in his *War Memoirs*, gives September 15 as the culminating date of the Battle of the Air. He tells how he visited the Operations Room of the R.A.F. that day and watched as the enemy squadrons poured over and ours went up to meet them until the moment came when he asked the Air Marshal, 'What other reserves have we?'

" 'There are none,' he answered, and reported afterwards how grave Mr. Churchill looked.

"Then another five minutes passed and 'it appeared the enemy were going home. The shifting of discs on the table showed a continuous eastward movement of German bombers and fighters. No new attack appeared. In another ten minutes the action was ended.' There seemed no reason why the Luftwaffe should have turned for home, just at the moment when victory was in their grasp.

"After the war, Air Chief Marshal Lord Dowding made this significant comment: 'Even during the battle one realized from day to day how much external support was coming in. At the end of the battle one had the feeling that there had been some special Divine intervention to alter some sequence of events which would otherwise have occurred.'"[3]

We must never underestimate the importance of our prayers, especially when their influence is not easy to see.

THOSE IN AUTHORITY

President Ronald Reagan had just finished giving a speech. He was almost at his limousine when he heard "Pop, pop, pop," like the sound of firecrackers. He was quickly hurled into the car with a secret service agent landing on top of him. He felt like the fall broke a rib. After he coughed, a blood soaked handkerchief evidenced a more severe injury.

Recovering after surgery in the hospital, he learned a bullet had flattened against the limousine then ricocheted, hitting his ribcage edgewise, stopping an inch from his heart. Three other men with him were severely injured.

He wrote in his diary, "Whatever happens now, I owe my life to God and will try to serve Him in every way I can."[4]

Many prayer warriors are committed to pray daily for our president. Events of that day, May 30, 1981, provide good evidence of the importance of those prayers.

When we think of those in authority over us, the most logical thoughts are of our United States president, the vice president, his cabinet, judges in the Supreme Court, and members of congress. This list can quickly expand to include our governor and state office holders; our mayor and local councilpersons. Since we are commanded to pray for these, we should make an effort to know who they are and how best to pray for them. Newspapers and the Holy Spirit will each help us when we pray.

School boards, teachers, and staff have important positions of authority over children. We can pray specifically as we are acquainted with teachers of family members.

Other world leaders include those who control international businesses and industries. We must also keep in our prayers those who control TV, newspapers, movies, other media, and entertainment in all its forms.

CLOSE TO HOME

Darrel and I frequently pray for those in authority over us, including those in the workplace. Over eleven years Darrel experienced the unusual transition of having more than a dozen bosses. With each new manager we prayed blessing for him and his family—especially praying, "May Your kingdom come and Your will be done in these lives."

We may not know the results of these prayers until we learn them in heaven.

PATTERNS AND PROMISES

- *I looked for a man among them who would build up the wall and stand before Me in the gap on behalf of the land so I would not have to destroy it, but I found none* (Ezekiel 22:30).

- *If My people, who are called by My name, will humble themselves and pray and seek My face and turn from their wicked ways, then will I hear from heaven and will forgive their sin and will heal their land. Now My eyes will be open and My ears attentive to the prayers offered in this place* (2 Chronicles 7:14-15).

- *In accordance with Your great love, forgive the sin of these people, just as You have pardoned them from the time they left Egypt until now. The Lord replied, "I have forgiven them, as you asked"* (Numbers 14:19-20).

- *Therefore, you kings, be wise; be warned, you rulers of the earth. Serve the Lord with fear and rejoice with trembling* (Psalm 2:10-11).

- *The God of Israel spoke, the Rock of Israel said to me: "When one rules over men in righteousness, when he rules in the fear of God, he is like the light of morning at sunrise on a cloudless morning, like the brightness after rain that brings the grass from the earth"* (2 Samuel 23:3-4).

- *If any of you lacks wisdom, he should ask God, who gives generously to all without finding fault and it will be given to him* (James 1:5).

PERSONAL PRAYER MANUAL

Title this divider "Nation/Authority." List by name those you are instructed to pray for in the preceding scriptures. There are many sources to tap for help. After elections the newspapers print lists of the new office holders, often including photos. I clipped a news photo of the Supreme Court justices and taped it on one page. It helps me visualize each person as I pray.

For years I have received the newsletter from Intercessors for America, a nondenominational resource that provides a national watch.[5] These are brief summaries of positive and negative events, legislation, and reports from across the nation to be included in both prayer and praise.

The monthly newsletter from the American Center for Law and Justice (ACLJ) is another excellent resource for intercessory prayer.[6] They are involved on many fronts providing legal defense where Christians and Christianity are being attacked, such as defending "one nation under God" in the flag salute.

I often use information provided in the American Family Association Journal to help me pray against anti-Christian social issues.[7] This is an excellent source of up-to-date news regarding morality vs. immorality and decadence in TV, movies, and books. It's also helpful to find sponsors listed.

SELF-EXAMINATION

1. Have I neglected to pray for those in authority?
2. Have I underestimated my influence through prayer in political affairs?
3. Would it make any difference to my nation if I started praying more earnestly?
4. Have I failed to see the news as a source of prayer prompting?

PRAYER

The following excellent prayer is from Bill Gothard's Basic Youth Conflicts material. The organization was renamed the Institute of Basic Life Principles.[8]

Heavenly Father, I thank You for our country, our Constitution and our leaders. I pray for our President and for every elected and appointed official who serves with him.

I pray that You will build a wall of protection around the marriage and family of every national, state and local official.

I pray that You will give them the wisdom and the courage to uphold our constitution which established a republic based on Your absolute laws; not a democracy based on the changing whims of human reasoning.

I pray that You will rebuke Satan for the deception of his lie that we can be "as gods" in deciding for ourselves what is right and what is wrong.

O Lord, May our leaders cast down every law, policy, and personal example which weakens marriages, families, or Your moral standards.

I pray that our leaders will understand and follow the principles of Your Word. May they realize that all authority comes from You, not the voters, and that one day they will stand before You to give an account of the power You gave to them.

I base this prayer on the promise of Your Word, that if I will humble myself, pray, seek Your face, and turn from my wicked ways, then You will hear from heaven, forgive my sin, and heal my land.

In the name and through the blood of the Lord Jesus Christ, I pray. Amen.

"We will see that if we do not confidently and aggressively pray for the sick, we have not recognized the comprehensive nature of Christ's victory over evil nor have we seen the comprehensive nature of our assignment as followers of Jesus."[8]

—Ken Blue

CHAPTER TWELVE

Healing and Wholeness

VERA'S TUMOR

Above my desk are the words, "The palest ink is stronger than the strongest memory." The Bible advises us to not forget the wonderful things God does for us, but to write them down and tell them to our children and our children's children. Vera's miracle is one of those.

At age ninety-one, Darrel's mother, Vera, was admitted to the hospital in great pain, jaundiced and dehydrated. On Friday, after her CT scan, the surgeon explained, "She has an infection in her biliary system and an obstruction of her bile duct. The scan showed a gallstone, but that isn't the problem. On the CT scan I saw a large tumor in the head of the pancreas pressing on the bile duct. With a tumor this size, removal is not an option. We could do a bypass to relieve the obstruction, but she would die from the cancer in 3 to 6 months."

"What would you do if she were your mother?" I questioned.

"I would keep her as comfortable as possible in the time she has left." He shook his head in sympathy.

Her cardiologist went into a longer explanation, but answered our question the same way. "Dying from pancreatic cancer is not pretty. I would keep her as comfortable as possible in the weeks she may have left."

With anxious hearts we attended a mission banquet at our church that night. At the end of the program, people with needs were encouraged to approach one of the missionaries, who would pray and anoint each with oil. Darrel went for prayer on Vera's behalf.

Pastor Mark Dalan, a young missionary preparing to leave for North Africa, prayed over Darrel who stood in proxy for his mother. He prayed boldly, "God, we ask you to remove the tumor and heal Vera."

Later, Darrel and I found ourselves praying small prayers. "Lord, move this tumor, shrink the tumor to relieve the pressure on the bile duct." When we listened to our prayers we felt guilty about our expectations. Our God is great, a God of miracles. We changed our prayers. "Lord, do a healing miracle in Vera's body."

On Monday, the family gathered in the cardiologist's office. He gave us the news. "The surgeon, the radiologist, and I looked at the CT scan again. Today we see no tumor. Our conclusion is the obstruction must be caused by gallstones. The surgeon wants to do surgery tomorrow."

After the extensive surgery on Tuesday, the surgeon spoke with us. "I examined the pancreas and I saw no evidence of a tumor."

"How did we get from where we were on Friday to where we are today?" I questioned.

"I can't explain it. I saw the CT scan myself, and I saw the tumor on Friday. On Monday, it wasn't there."

Vera came home from the hospital in three days and recovered rapidly. She lived six more healthy years.

Historically, unbelievers attempt to explain away miracles. Yet anyone who tries to explain away Vera's miracle must conclude she was in the hands of three careless doctors. This is not the case. All three have fine reputations.

Darrel and I find it easy to believe God intervened in answer to the many prayers on Vera's behalf.

HEALTHY PLANS

The Bible records numerous examples of healing accomplished by Jesus. He never refused anyone who requested healing. A survey of God's relationship with His chosen ones throughout the Bible reveals His desire for our health and wholeness. One of His names, Jehovah Rophe, means "I am the Lord who heals you" (Exodus 15:26).

GOOD AND BAD SHEPHERDS

In the well-loved 23rd Psalm, David describes the Lord as the Good Shepherd who provides green pastures, quiet waters, goodness and mercy for those in His charge.

Ezekiel records a prophecy from God condemning the shepherds of Israel. *"You have not strengthened the weak or healed the sick or bound up the injured. You have not brought back the strays or searched for the lost. You have ruled them harshly and brutally"* (Ezekiel 34:4). That's a graphic list of what a good shepherd is not.

Jesus speaks of himself, *"I am the Good Shepherd. The Good Shepherd lays down His life for the sheep"* (John 10:11). From Him we can expect the opposite of bad shepherding. He will strengthen the weak, heal the sick, bind up the injured, bring back strays, and search for the lost.

VIEWS ON DISEASE

The Bible describes instances where God used disease and death to punish people who were rebellious and disobedient. Frequently, however, this is not the case. Consider the source of Job's afflictions. God gave Satan permission to test Job's faith through physical pain.

In another instance, the disciples asked Jesus about a man blind from birth. *"Who sinned, this man or his parents?"*

Jesus gave an unexpected answer. *"Neither this man nor his parents sinned, but this happened so that the work of God might be displayed in his life"* (John 9:1-3).

Dr. Ken Blue states, "Jesus never preached surrender to sickness and neither should we. There are many among us who could be healed if only we would pray for them. I am someone who for years suffered chronic back pain, having accepted it as a divine means of taming my pride. Only after I was delivered of this erroneous notion was I effectively prayed for and completely healed. Our theology must sometimes be healed before our bodies can be."[1]

Many questions remain unanswered in the realm of healing, but it's apparent God wants us to seek Him as the source of health for ourselves and others as well. Our responsibility is to ask. God's answer may be, "Yes," "Not yet," or "No, I have a different plan." God isn't our heavenly errand boy. Remember, even Jesus prayed, *"Not My will but Thine"* (Luke 22:42 KJV).

FAITH

Faith accompanies healing and operates by degrees: Great faith, small faith and no faith. The eighth chapter of Matthew gives an account of a Roman centurion who came to Jesus on behalf of his sick servant. When Jesus offered to go to his house, the centurion said it wasn't necessary. He understood how one in authority speaks and the command is carried out.

When Jesus heard this, He was astonished and said to those following Him, "I tell you the truth, I have not found anyone in Israel with such great faith." Then Jesus said to the centurion, "Go! It will be done just as you believed it would." And his servant was healed at the very hour (Matthew 8:10,13).

This illustrates the importance of the faith of the intercessor when someone intercedes for another. We know nothing of the faith of the servant, the one who received the healing.

When a blind man stopped Jesus as he traveled along the road and asked that his blindness be healed, *Jesus said to him, "Receive your sight; your faith has healed you"* (Luke 18:42).

Things were much different for Jesus in his hometown. *He could not do any miracles there, except lay His hands on a few sick people and heal them. And He was amazed at their lack of faith* (Mark 6:5-6).

Two of the gifts of the Spirit listed in 1 Corinthians 12 are important to consider here. The gifts of healing and the gift of faith often work together. We are told to *eagerly desire spiritual gifts* (1 Corinthians 14:1).

CHRIS AND GUILLON BARRÉ SYNDROME

Thirty-three-year-old Chris awakened unable to use his hands and arms. His legs and feet were almost useless. After he was transported to the hospital, a spinal tap ruled out polio or meningitis. The doctors diagnosed Guillon Barré syndrome, which affects the spinal cord and nerves. Within 24 hours Chris was completely paralyzed from the neck down.

His lungs quickly experienced the effects of the disease. The vital capacity of his lungs dropped from normal 5 to 1.4. He was unable to cough and clear the accumulating congestion. After twelve fearful days he was in danger of respiratory failure.

His mother, Norma, was suddenly impressed to go to the hospital. "I felt drawn to the hospital. I found that Chris' left lung had collapsed and he had developed pneumonia. His vital capacity fell to .95."

Chris' wife, Margaret, and a friend were praying for him when Norma arrived. "When I touched Chris' feet and joined their prayers, my hands became so hot I felt like there should be blisters on them."

Margaret replied, "Norma, I think the Holy Spirit is leading you to pray and lay your hands on Chris for healing—like in the New Testament."

When Norma placed her hands on the area of the collapsed lung, her hands and arms shook uncontrollably. She talked quietly to God. "Thank you for the healing You promise in Your Word. Thank you for the blood of Jesus that protects us. Lord, heal Chris. Take this terrible disease from his body." She continued to pray until finally there was a sense of clearness and peace in her mind.

The next day when Norma returned to Chris' room she was amazed to see Chris sitting in a chair. He told her, "I can lift my torso up in bed, bend my waist in several directions, and my lungs are clearing. Look, I can turn my hands over."

Chris' recovery was so rapid he left the hospital in a few short days. He continued to experience weakness for many weeks. Chris, Margaret, and Norma have no doubt if God had not provided a healing miracle, Chris wouldn't have survived.

Norma said, "After this incredible encounter with the flow of God's healing power, I discovered Matthew 1:17, *He took our infirmities and carried our diseases.* I knew Jesus took our sins, but I didn't realize he took our infirmities, too."

PATTERNS AND PROMISES

- *And wherever He went—into villages, towns or countryside— they placed the sick in the marketplaces. They begged Him to let them touch even the edge of His cloak, and all who touched Him were healed* (Mark 6:56).
- *The Spirit of the Sovereign Lord is on Me, because the Lord has anointed Me to preach good news to the poor. He has sent Me to bind up the brokenhearted, to proclaim freedom for the captives and release from darkness for the prisoners, to proclaim the year of the Lord's favor and the day of vengeance of our God, to comfort all who mourn, and provide for those who grieve in Zion—to bestow on them a crown of beauty instead of ashes, the oil of gladness instead of mourning, and a garment of praise instead of a spirit of despair. They will be called oaks of righteousness, a planting of the Lord for the display of His splendor* (Isaiah 61:1-3).
- *Praise the Lord, O my soul, and forget not all His benefits— who forgives all your sins and heals all your diseases* (Psalm 103:2).
- *Is any one of you sick? He should call the elders of the church to pray over him and anoint him with oil in the name of the Lord. And the prayer offered in faith will make the sick person well; the Lord will raise him up. If he has sinned, he will be forgiven. Therefore confess your sins to each other and pray for*

each other so that you may be healed. The prayer of a righteous man is powerful and effective (James 5:14-16).

- *And these signs will accompany those who believe: In My name they will drive out demons; they will speak in new tongues; they will pick up snakes with their hands; and when they drink deadly poison, it will not hurt them at all; they will place their hands on sick people, and they will get well* (Mark 16:17-18).

- *Ask and it will be given to you; seek and you will find; knock and the door will be opened to you. For everyone who asks receives; he who seeks finds; and to him who knocks, the door will be opened. Which of you, if his son asks for bread, will give him a stone? Or if he asks for a fish, will give him a snake? If you, then, though you are evil, know how to give good gifts to your children, how much more will your Father in heaven give good gifts to those who ask Him* (Matthew 7:7-11)!

- *"But I will restore you to health and heal your wounds," declares the Lord...*(Jeremiah 30:17).

PERSONAL PRAYER MANUAL

Label this divider "Healing." Collect other scriptures related to healing for additional encouragement to pray. Here you will list all those you know who are in need of healing. Personalize Scripture passages as you pray. Remember to ask the Holy Spirit for guidance in how to pray. Be sure to date your entries and again when the answer becomes apparent.

I have often said, "Waiting to see the answers to our prayers is much like being pregnant. We know a baby is coming, but there's no joy like seeing the new arrival." We know God hears our prayers and we know He answers. Sometimes I look at my list and thank God for His provision, even though the answers are not yet visible.

SELF EXAMINATION

1. Have I examined God's Word enough to know with assurance His desire to heal and care for His loved ones?

2. Am I willing to be persistent, like the woman who cried out to the unjust judge day and night? (Luke 18:1-9).
3. Am I confident that the Lord calls each of us to be intercessors and use His authority?

Dear Heavenly Father, Good Shepherd, Jehovah Rophe, how good to know Your Name is above every name—even names like cancer, heart disease, AIDS, and blindness. Thank You for Your promise to heal the broken hearted and bind up their wounds. Thank You for Jesus' example that wherever He went He healed all who came to Him. Thank You, too, for the assurance that Jesus is the same, yesterday, today, and forever. Fill my heart with compassion for those in need of healing. Holy Spirit, help me pray for those You have placed in my life. I pray in the precious name of Jesus my Savior and Lord.

"Spiritual warfare is not a fragment of Christianity. It is the whole of the Christian experience. It encompasses everything we do. To be a Christian is to be a spiritual warrior. To be a spiritual warrior is to walk consistently and victoriously through life with Christ at our side."[2]

—Dean Sherman

CHAPTER THIRTEEN

Deliver Us from Evil

RECOGNIZE THE ENEMY

God gives us power to be overcomers, to be victors over the enemy. To obtain this victory, we must recognize the enemy and know our weapons against him. We would have to eliminate a large portion of the Bible if we tried to deny his existence. In the New Testament alone there are over 150 references to Satan, the devil, demons, and evil spirits.

We first meet Satan in Genesis when he deceived Adam and Eve. We see the end of his reign of terror in Revelation when he is cast into the lake of fire. In Jesus' life and ministry He confronted Satan and his demons many times, always showing God's victorious power over this foe. Ezekiel 28 describes Lucifer, the beautiful being Satan was when God created him. *You were the model of perfection, full of wisdom and perfect in beauty.* In Isaiah 14 we read the reason for his expulsion from heaven. He said, *"I will make myself like the Most High."* He persuaded one third of God's angels to follow him and serve him.

Satan, the devil, is not a power opposite of God, but of the Archangel Michael. When C. S. Lewis was asked whether he believed in devils, he replied, "I do. That is to say, I believe in angels, and I believe some of these, by the abuse of their free will, have become enemies of God and, as a corollary, to us. These we may call devils. They do not differ in nature from good angels, but their nature is depraved."[1]

ARMOR TO STAND

If we weren't engaged in a battle, we wouldn't need armor. But we are instructed to *Put on the full armor of God so that you can take your stand against the devil's schemes. For our struggle is not against flesh and blood, but against the rulers, against the authorities, against the powers of this dark world and against the spiritual forces of evil in heavenly realms* (Ephesians 6:11-12). We're given a long list of the whole armor of God for believers: the belt of truth; the breastplate of righteousness; the gospel of peace; the shield of faith; the helmet of salvation and the sword of the Spirit. Examining this list, we realize Jesus is our armor. He is our salvation, righteousness, truth, peace, the Word of God, and the Author of our faith.

God made us joint heirs with Jesus, the heirs of His awesome power (Romans 8:17). In Matthew 28:18 we read, *Then Jesus came to them and said, "All authority in heaven and on earth has been given to me."*

After Jesus' baptism, the Spirit led him into the desert where he was tempted by the devil. Jesus answered every challenge from Satan with the Word of God saying, "It is written…"(Luke 4:1-10). He gave us a powerful example to follow.

BONDAGE

Spiritual bondage can take many forms. Jesus set free a woman with a severely deformed back *whom Satan had bound for eighteen years* (Luke 13:16). Jesus cast out demons that manifested their presence with symptoms like insanity, epilepsy, physical illness, and deafness.

The Holy Spirit equips us with the gift of discerning of spirits to help us recognize the enemy and his ways. God's Spirit opens our spiritual eyes to see things our physical eyes can't. He even helps us know how to pray.

The following Scripture passages will build your faith to claim victory over the enemy.

PATTERNS AND PROMISES

- *The seventy returned with joy saying, "Lord, even the demons submit to us in your name."*
  And He said to them, "I saw Satan fall like lightning from heaven. Behold, I have given you authority to tread upon snakes and scorpions, and over all the power of the enemy; and nothing will harm you. Nevertheless, do not rejoice in this, that the spirits submit to you; but rejoice that your names are written in heaven" (Luke 10:17-20 RSV).
- *The weapons we fight with are not the weapons of the world. On the contrary, they have divine power to demolish strongholds. We demolish arguments and every pretension that sets itself up against the knowledge of God, and we take captive every thought to make it obedient to Christ* (2 Corinthians 10:4-5).
- *You, dear children, are from God and have overcome them, because the One who is in you is greater than the one who is in the world* (1 John 4:4).
- *The reason the Son of God appeared was to destroy the devil's work* (1 John 3:8).
- *They overcame him by the blood of the Lamb and by the word of their testimony* (Revelation 12:11).
- *Submit yourselves, then, to God. Resist the devil, and he will flee from you. Come near to God and He will come near to you* (James 4:7-8).
- *I tell you the truth, whatever you bind on earth will be bound in heaven, and whatever you loose on earth will be loosed in heaven* (Matthew 18:18).

MILITANT BELIEVERS

"God does not intend you to be passively trustful; He wants you to be militantly believing! He wants you to storm the very gates of

Hades and rout the devil. He wants you to dislodge the forces of Satan from their long-entrenched positions."[2] In his book *Touch the World through Prayer,* Wesley Duewel makes several other strong, encouraging observations. He reminds us Satan and his demons do not want us to learn the secrets of prayer. They fear our prayers.

"Spiritual warfare is a life lived. It is embracing the truth and living daily, aware of the enemy and committed to God. It is knowing that God has left it up to us. If we do not drive back the powers of darkness, they will not be driven back. If we do not rebuke the enemy, he will not be rebuked. If we do not reduce the evil in the world, it will continue to grow."[3]

Several years ago I participated in a women's Bible study on prayer where we followed a study guide. When we came to the chapter on spiritual warfare the leader suggested we should bypass the part dealing with demons. I experienced an unusual pounding of my heart and sensed this was a leading from the Holy Spirit.

I spoke up. "I think it's important that we cover this teaching and not omit it." My palpitations increased. My arms and hands tingled and both hands had a visible tremor.

The leader asked, "Marge, what do you want us to do?"

"It's not what I want us to do," I replied. "It's what God wants us to do. Lets proceed and read all the scriptures. We can skip making comments if you'd prefer."

That's just what we did. Even in a group of Christians, there were those who had little interest in studying the enemy and how to defeat him.

No Clear Division

In reviewing some of the scriptures on healing, it is clear there may be an overlapping of prayers for healing and prayers of release from the power of the enemy. Recall that my prayer for healing from symptoms of the flu before flying to Jamaica included binding the power of Satan. The resulting healing included far more than I asked for. I was set free from recurring headaches and severe motion sickness.

I once shared the needs of a Christian friend with a group at Bible study. Mandy was so overcome with a desire to sleep she was barely able to function. When we prayed for her, we felt led to pray, "Satan, we bind you and everything you have brought on Mandy. In the Name of Jesus we command you to leave her. She is God's property." Mandy later reported a remarkable change. She was physically active again.

I recall a time when a severe depression settled over me. Darrel telephoned my prayer partner and handed me the phone where I lay in bed. Carol prayed for me and took authority over the enemy. Before long the darkness lifted.

Many Christians talk about their authority. They sing about it. But they don't use it. We must recognize the important difference between having authority and using it.

METHODS OF EXERCISING OUR AUTHORITY[4]

1. The Name of Jesus as a Weapon.
   In My Name they will drive out demons (Mark 16:17).
   The Name of Jesus carries with it all the victory of the cross and resurrection.
2. The Word of God in Warfare.
   Take…the sword of the Spirit, which is the Word of God (Ephesians 6:17).
   Jesus used the Word of God in the wilderness when dealing with Satan, and we, too, need to speak out Scripture, using it as a mighty weapon.
3. The Power of the Holy Spirit.
   Jesus said in Matthew 12:28, "*I drive out demons by the Spirit of God.*" If He did it by the power of the Holy Spirit, then we also need to *pray in the Spirit on all occasions* in order to drive back and break down the powers of the enemy (Ephesians 6:18).
4. The Blood of Jesus.
   They overcame him by the blood of the Lamb…(Revelation 12:11).

The declaration of His blood has a powerful effect on the enemy. It brings that defeat into each and every situation— freshly applying it for this time and place. There really is power in the blood.

5. Telling the Truth.
   They overcame him…by the word of their testimony (Revelation 12:11).

First, it's a declaration of the great acts and character of God. The devil's purpose is to discredit God. Then we must proclaim the positive truth about ourselves: who we are in Christ. We can proclaim, "I am washed by Jesus' blood. I am a new creature in Christ. I am more than a conqueror." This testimony of truth will shatter the intimidation and accusations of the enemy.

DELIVERANCE

Many authors have written entire books helping Christians understand their role in proclaiming and establishing Christ's victory over the enemy. It's important to read one of these to see the big picture. When it comes to spiritual warfare, if it's not in the Bible, be cautious.

In countries where the worship of demons is common, Christian workers frequently observe demon possession. In western countries we see more of those who practice occult activities, seek to have their fortunes told, or try to contact spirit guides. They are opening themselves to demonic activity.

Corrie ten Boom told of a conversation with young woman, May, who had visited a fortuneteller. "May said, 'But I did not believe in it. I did it only for fun.'"

Corrie replied, "May, Suppose you were a soldier during war, and you had to reconnoiter certain terrain. By mistake you fell into the enemy's hands by entering his territory. Do you think that it would help if you then said, 'O excuse me, please, it was not my intention to come here, I just came by mistake'? Once you are on their terrain, you are at their mercy."[5]

A dear friend and her mother were reading a novel based on demon warfare that was highly touted in the Christian and secular world. Here is my friend's testimony.

"I hated the book and laid it aside many times. Yet it held such a horrible fascination for me I felt compelled to read to the end.

"Mom's experience with the book was even more intense. She awakened one morning with flu-like symptoms and running a high temperature. For two days she felt as if she were being attacked by the demons in the story. It wasn't until we removed the book from our house and prayed for God to banish all taint of evil that the peace of Christ returned to us and our home."

On the other hand, when I read the same novel, I had a very different experience. I was impressed with the mighty warrior angels and their frequent comment about their power being directly related to the prayers and praise of God's people. They hoped the battle wasn't imminent because there were not sufficient prayers from God's people to erect a prayer shield. The progress of the prayer cover was referred to several times. By the time I finished the book, I went to my knees to pray.

Like so many things in life, the same thing can be used for good or evil. That's why we are cautioned many times in the Scriptures to *watch* and *take heed.*

The Holy Spirit equips us with the gift of discerning of spirits to know when and how to pray for those under the influence of demons. The following from the *Handbook of Spiritual Warfare* by Dr. Ed Murphy[6] is a concise list to assist Christians in the ministry of deliverance.

REQUIREMENTS FOR DELIVERANCE

1. Be assured of salvation through personal faith in the Lord Jesus Christ.
2. Humble yourself before God. Be totally open and honest with Him.
3. Confess and renounce the sin of your family line.
4. Confess and renounce your own sins.

5. Choose to forgive everyone who has hurt, rejected, or offended you, especially those who have injured you the most deeply (an act of faith and obedience; your emotions have nothing to do with the matter).
6. Ask God to forgive, redeem, and cleanse those who have hurt you. Desire (by faith) their salvation and spiritual well-being.
7. Commit the totality of your life to the absolute lordship of the Lord Jesus Christ.
8. Speak out against Satan and his demons, declaring they no longer have any place in your life. Their sin grounds have been removed. They must now leave your life and not return.

Personal Prayer Manual

Title this divider "Warfare." In these pages you may list several specific addictions: alcohol, drugs, gambling, gluttony, TV, pornography, and sexual addiction. By grouping together names of people with the same problem, it is easy to pray for them all at one time. This is a good place to name those who have contemplated suicide. Those who have come under the darkness and error of cults and false religions also belong on these pages.

Collect additional Scripture examples of deliverance from Satan. Also add scriptures reminding you of your authority as a joint heir with Jesus.

Self Examination

1. Am I guilty of ignoring the power of the enemy who comes to steal, kill, and destroy?
2. Have I underestimated the authority that has been delegated to me?
3. Am I willing to follow Jesus' example and be open to the leading of the Holy Spirit in standing in His victory and defeating the enemy?

Almighty God, Loving Father, Jehovah-Nissi our victory banner, thank You for the atoning death of Jesus and His defeat of Satan. Remind me, Lord, though he prowls around like a roaring lion, he is a defeated enemy. Open my eyes, Holy Spirit, to discern his work and to use the authority given me to overcome him. Help me hide Your Word in my heart that I might be resourceful with the Sword of the Spirit. Lord, instruct me how to fast as a tool against Satan's wiles. Use me, Lord, to help set others free from demonic influence. Thank You, that You have not given me a spirit of fear, but of power, love, and a sound mind. Help me be your faithful servant. I pray in Jesus' Name and under the protection of His blood. Amen.

"The prayer closet is the arena which produces the overcomer."[7]

—Paul Billheimer

CHAPTER FOURTEEN

Setting Prisoners Free

BIBLICAL PRISONERS

God's concern for those in prison is an important provision in the big picture of His compassionate care. The experiences of several prisoners are found in the Bible, along with God's involvement with each. In Genesis 39 we read how Joseph, after being sold as a slave by his jealous brothers, was a servant in the house of one of Pharaoh's officials. When his master's wife falsely accused him of trying to seduce her, Joseph was put into prison. While he was in prison, the Lord was with him. He showed Joseph kindness and granted him favor in the eyes of the prison warden. After several dramatic events (and more than two years) Joseph was released from prison and put in charge of Pharaoh's palace.

The prophet Jeremiah spoke the words of the Lord of the impending disaster coming to the people of Judah unless they turned from their wickedness. His unpopular message caused him to be beaten and imprisoned, first in a cell, then the courtyard of the guard. Later he was lowered into an abandoned cistern, where he sank into the muddy bottom, and was left to starve. He was rescued and returned to the courtyard of the guard. After the predicted fall of Jerusalem, Jeremiah was freed from his chains, given provisions and his freedom (Jeremiah 37-40). He continued to speak prophecies from God.

The book of Daniel relates two occurrences of God's miraculous delivery of prisoners. After King Nebuchadnezzar had constructed a ninety-foot high golden image, he commanded, "*Whoever does not fall down and worship will immediately be thrown into a blazing furnace*" (Daniel 3:6). When Shadrach, Meshach, and Abednego refused to bow to the image they were thrown into a furnace heated seven times hotter than usual.

The king was amazed at what he saw. "*Wasn't it three men we tied up and threw into the fire? Look, I see four men walking around in the fire, unbound and unharmed, and the fourth looks like a son of the gods.*"

When they were released, the fire had not harmed their bodies, nor was their hair singed. Their robes were not scorched and there was no smell of fire on them. The king recognized what he had seen. "*Praise be to the God of Shadrach, Meshach and Abednego, who has sent His angel and rescued His servants*" (Daniel 3:28).

In a plan to entrap Daniel, the advisors of King Darius encouraged him to issue a decree that anyone who prayed to any god or man during the next thirty days would be thrown into the lions' den. Daniel ignored the decree and continued to pray and give thanks to God just as he had done before. The king reluctantly gave the order and Daniel was thrown into the lions' den.

In the morning the king hurried to the den and called to Daniel who answered him. "*O king, live forever! My God sent His angel, and He shut the mouths of the lions. They have not hurt me...*" (Daniel 6:21).

John the Baptist was beheaded in prison. He had spoken of Jesus, "*He must become greater and I must become less*" (John 4:30).

An account in the book of Acts tells how the jealous Sadducees arrested some apostles and put them in jail. But during the night an angel of the Lord opened the doors of the jail and brought them out (Acts 5:19).

After Paul and Silas had delivered a slave girl from a fortune telling spirit, her owners became angry. They realized their hopes of making money with her were gone. They had Paul and Silas flogged and imprisoned, with their feet fastened in stocks. *About midnight Paul and Silas were praying and singing hymns to God.... Suddenly there was such a violent earthquake that the foundations of the prison were shaken. At once all the prison doors flew open, and everybody's chains came loose* (Acts 16:25). Subsequently, the frightened jailer believed in Jesus. He took the disciples to his home, fed them, and cared for their wounds.

Paul wrote many of the New Testament letters while in prison.

The apostle John wrote the book of Revelation in exile.

God still changes the lives of prisoners. Charles Colson wrote of his dramatic encounter with Christ when he was involved in one of the greatest governmental crises in American history: the Watergate scandal and the downfall of President Richard Nixon. Catherine Marshall is quoted on the jacket of Colson's book, *Born Again*[1]. "As I read these absorbing pages I was supplied with solid encouragement and hope, for if God can still reach down and reverse the direction of a modern man's life as he did with Charles Colson, then not a one of us or our families are beyond His reach."

The poor choices we make can land us in prisons with bars on the windows and locks on the doors. They can also keep us in invisible prisons that hinder us from being all God wants us to be. Consider the limitations we place on ourselves when we allow certain attitudes to rule us: anger, fear, guilt, shame, jealousy, lying, pride, and unforgiveness. They not only hinder our relationships with our family and friends, but most of all, they also hamper or even obstruct our relationship with God.

HUNGRY FOR HOPE

One day I visited with three young women in jail and guessed they might be prostitutes. Each was so hungry for hope—concern for a child, estrangement from parents. I gave them each a small blue New Testament with the plan of salvation printed inside the back cover, and a list of specific helps in the front. We read together some encouraging scriptures and prayed that the women would find mercy in the court. They received God's promises with smiles of gratitude. They were encouraged to hear that Jesus loved each one of them and her family.

Another day in prison I visited with a young Haitian girl, a Christian with a French Bible. Using my English New Testament and her Bible, we bridged the language barrier by turning to the same scriptures. I prayed that she would go before a just judge and God would have mercy on her. She hugged me when I left so I would know how grateful she was for the encouragement.

God offers encouragement for those in prison, whether visible or invisible—even those of our own making. The following scriptures will jumpstart your prayers for those in prison.

PATTERNS AND PROMISES

- *May the groans of the prisoners come before You; by the strength of Your arm preserve those condemned to die* (Psalm 79:11).
- *The Lord looked down from His sanctuary on high, from heaven He viewed the earth, to hear the groans of the prisoners and release those condemned to death* (Psalm 102:19-20).
- *But He took note of their distress when He heard their cry; for their sake He remembered His covenant and out of His great love He relented. He caused them to be pitied by all who held them captive* (Psalm 106:44-46).
- *This is what the Lord says: "In the time of my favor I will answer you…to say to the captives, 'Come out,' and to those in darkness, 'Be free'"* (Isaiah 49:8a-9a).
- *But thus saith the Lord, "Even the captives of the mighty shall be taken away, and the prey of the terrible shall be delivered: for I will contend with him that contendeth with thee, and I will save thy children"* (Isaiah 49:25 KJV).
- *The Spirit of the Lord is on Me, because He has anointed Me to preach good news to the poor. He has sent Me to proclaim freedom for the prisoners and recovery of sight for the blind, to release the oppressed…*(Luke 4:18).
- *Then the King will say to those on His right, "Come, you who are blessed by my Father; take your inheritance, the kingdom*

prepared for you since the creation of the world. For I was hungry and you gave Me something to eat, I was thirsty and you gave Me something to drink, I was a stranger and you invited Me in, I needed clothes and you clothed Me, I was sick and you looked after Me, I was in prison and you came to visit Me" (Matthew 25:34-36).

Personal Prayer Manual

Title this divider "Prisoners." List those you are concerned with who are in physical prisons. There is no clear division in the work of the enemy whether the prison is visible or invisible. Some of the same people you listed in the "Deliver Us from Evil" portion of your prayer manual may be included here also.

This is a good place to include the individuals and organizations that actively minister to prisoners. The largest and most successful ministry is Prison Fellowship International, which was founded by Chuck Colson.

Remember to collect additional scriptures here to further assist you in praying God's Word.

Self Examination

1. Have I neglected the privilege and responsibility to pray for those in prison?
2. Do I read the newspaper, watch the TV news, and read Christian newsletters with an awareness of these as resources for prayer needs?
3. Have I forgotten the opportunity I have to minister to Jesus as I pray for prisoners? Remember, He said, *"I was in prison and you visited Me."*

Heavenly Father, I thank you that one of Your Names is Jehovah Jireh, God's provision shall be seen. I come to intercede for those in prison, that Your kingdom will come and Your will may be done in their lives. May they know the conviction and fellowship of the Holy Spirit. Provide Your light to shatter their darkness and Your truth to dispel their error. Strengthen, encourage, and protect all those who minister in prisons. In Jesus' precious name I pray. Amen.

"When we pray the pure Word of God we open ourselves to pure faith, and we cannot help but get involved in pure prayers."[2]

—Judson Cornwall

CHAPTER FIFTEEN

Faith and Fasting

FAITH IS ESSENTIAL

The measure of our faith determines the intensity of our prayers. If we have faith to believe that God keeps His promises, our prayers increase in power in direct proportion to our knowledge of His promises.

The eleventh chapter of Hebrews is known as the faith chapter because it lists many Old Testament people and the miraculous events that occurred because of their faith. It also offers a good definition of faith.

- *Now faith is being sure of what we hope for and certain of what we do not see. This is what the ancients were commended for. By faith we understand that the universe was formed at God's command, so that what is seen was not made out of what was visible* (Hebrews 11:1-3).
- *And without faith it is impossible to please God, because anyone who comes to Him must believe that He exists and that He rewards those who earnestly seek Him* (Hebrews 11:6).

Remember how Abraham trusted God and His promises so absolutely that he was willing to offer his son as a sacrifice. Consider how ridiculous Noah's ark-building must have looked to those with no faith in God.

We can't generate our own faith no matter how hard we try. Faith is one of the many gifts provided by God. Jesus spoke of people with little faith and those who had great faith. God's Word instructs us and builds our faith.

- *Consequently, faith comes from hearing the message, and the message is heard through the Word of Christ* (Romans 10:17).
- *For it is by grace you have been saved, through faith—and this not from yourselves, it is the gift of God—not by works, so that no one can boast* (Ephesians 2:8).
- *But when the Holy Spirit controls our lives He will produce this kind of fruit in us: love, joy, peace, patience, kindness, goodness, faithfulness, gentleness and self-control.* (Galatians 5:22-23 TLB).
- *Now to each one the manifestation of the Spirit is given for the common good. To one there is given through the Spirit the message of wisdom, to another the message of knowledge by means of the same Spirit, to another faith by the same Spirit...*(1 Corinthians 12:7-9).
- *We live by faith, not by sight* (2 Corinthians 5:7).
- *Be on your guard; stand firm in the faith; be men of courage; be strong. Do everything in love* (1 Corinthians 16:13-14).

Many who came to Jesus displayed determined faith. The woman who had been sick for twelve years with bleeding knew in her spirit that she needed only to touch Jesus to be healed. Jesus spoke to her, *"Take heart, daughter, your faith has healed you"* (Matthew 9:22).

In the chapter on healing I gave an example of great faith. It is worth repeating. Jesus spoke of the great faith of a Roman centurion who requested healing for his servant who was at home. The centurion refused to inconvenience Jesus with a visit to his house. He could see a parallel between his own authority over those in his command and the spiritual authority of Jesus. He knew Jesus had only to speak and his servant would be healed. Jesus said to him, *"Go! It will be done just as you believed it would"* (Matthew 8:13). To His disciples He said, *"I have not found anyone in Israel with such great faith"* (Matthew 8:10).

The Bible is saturated with examples of people who took action as a result of a reality which was yet unseen. Their resource was faith in the living God Who keeps His promises. Faith always increases under the right circumstances, which includes reading the Bible.

Faith and trust are synonymous. Under the heading of faith in Nave's Topical Bible we find many scriptures that speak of trust.

- *Trust in the Lord with all your heart and lean not unto your own understanding; in all your ways acknowledge Him and He will make your paths straight* (Proverbs 3:5-6).
- *Thou wilt keep him in perfect peace whose mind is stayed on Thee: because he trusteth in Thee* (Isaiah 26:3 KJV).

CHILDLIKE FAITH

In the days before mandatory safety seats for children, our granddaughter Holly, age two, gave us a lesson in faith. In the front seat of our car with a seat belt across her lap, she sat on a makeshift arrangement of a folded blanket between Darrel and me. She wasn't comfortable.

Darrel announced, "Holly, I'm going to stop at a store and buy you a special seat, just to keep in Bopee's car so we'll always have it ready for you."

Bright eyed and expectant, Holly looked at him and exclaimed, "Oh thank you, Bopee!" She was as excited as though she already had it. She knew her grandpa was good for his promise.

Our son, Larry, planned a move to a new home. When he took his four-year-old son, Nathaniel, to look at the yard, Larry explained, "Grandpa will put a swing set here just for you."

Nathaniel responded with a bear hug. "Will it have one of those things where two people ride?" He knew the promise was good, and, in his mind, already fulfilled.

When grandson, little Darrel, was a toddler he loved to follow his Grandpa Darrel around the house. Grandpa busied himself assembling a complicated bunk bed set, and little Darrel kept getting in the way. Finally, grandpa put on a backpack designed to carry a child. With little Darrel on his back, Grandpa Darrel finished the project and the toddler was content. He was as close to his grandpa as he could get. This is a good visual image of the scripture that tells us to *draw near to God and He will draw near to you* (James 4:8a RSV).

Surely this kind of attitude and faith was what Jesus had in mind when he said, "*I tell you the truth, anyone who will not receive the kingdom of God like a little child will never enter it*" (Luke 18:17).

FASTING

By His example and His word, Jesus endorsed fasting. This is an arena that receives little mention in today's churches. Jesus, however, didn't say, "If you fast." He said, "*When you fast, do not look somber as the hypocrites do, for they disfigure their faces to show men they are fasting. I tell you the truth, they have received their reward in full. But when you fast, put oil on your head and wash your face, so that it will not be obvious to men that you are fasting, but only to your Father, who is unseen; and your Father, who sees what is done in secret, will reward you*" (Matthew 6:16-18).

Gordon Lindsay said, "Fasting is the master key by which the impossible becomes possible. But humility and repentance and sincerity of heart hold the key to fasting that is recognized by God."[1]

BIBLICAL FASTS

Historical records of the Bible reveal many instances when a national fast was called and disaster was averted as a result. Prayer, confession of sin, and reading the Scriptures usually accompanied it.

King Jehoshaphat, alarmed at the mighty army coming against him, proclaimed a national fast. Following a prayer by the king, a prophet spoke by the Spirit of the Lord and told of the victory awaiting them the next day. *"Do not be afraid or discouraged because of this vast army. For the battle is not yours, but God's. You will not have to fight this battle. Take up your positions; stand firm and see the deliverance the Lord will give you, O Judah and Jerusalem. Do not be afraid; do not be discouraged. Go out to face them tomorrow and the Lord will be with you"* (2 Chronicles 20:15-17).

When the Israelites were given permission to return to Jerusalem from their long captivity in Babylon, they were allowed to take with them all the articles of worship that had been removed from the temple. They were concerned about robbers who might attack them on their journey.

Ezra, the priest, recorded this account: *There by the Ahava Canal, I proclaimed a fast, so that we might humble ourselves before our God and ask Him for a safe journey for us and our children, with all our possessions. I was ashamed to ask the king for soldiers and horsemen to protect us from enemies on the road, because we had told the king, "The good hand of our God is on everyone who looks to Him, but His great anger is against all who forsake Him." So we fasted and petitioned our God about this, and He answered our prayer* (Ezra 8:21-23).

When Queen Esther heard of the plot to annihilate all the Jews in the land on a single day, she told her advisor, Mordecai, *"Go, gather all the Jews who are in Susa and fast for me. Do not eat or drink for three days, night or day. I and my maids will fast as you do. When this is done, I will go to the king, even though it is against the law. And if I perish, I perish"* (Esther 4:16). The fast resulted in a great victory for the Jews over their enemies.

Examples of fasting by individuals include Nehemiah and Daniel. Nehemiah was cupbearer to the king in Babylon. He heard the report that *those who survived the exile and are back in the province are in great trouble and disgrace. The wall of Jerusalem is broken down, and its gates have been burned with fire,* he sat down and wept. *"For some days I mourned and fasted and prayed before the God of heaven"* (Nehemiah 1:3-4).

Following this he found favor with the king who gave him permission to journey to Jerusalem to rebuild the walls.

When Daniel studied the Scriptures that included the Word of the Lord given to Jeremiah the prophet, he understood that the desolation of Jerusalem would last seventy years. This news grieved him. He recorded, *So I turned to the Lord and pleaded with him in prayer and petition, in fasting and in sackcloth and ashes.* He ends his long prayer of repentance with these words: *"We do not make requests of You because we are righteous, but because of Your great mercy. O Lord, listen! O Lord, forgive! O Lord, hear and act! For Your sake, O my God, do not delay, because Your city and Your people bear your Name"* (Daniel 9:3,18b).

Daniel recorded many visions from God.

The apostles and church leaders fasted for wisdom and guidance in the affairs of the church. *While they were worshiping the Lord and fasting, the Holy Spirit said, "Set apart for Me Barnabas and Saul for the work to which I have called them." So after they had fasted and prayed, they placed their hands on them and sent them off* (Acts 13:2-3).

The two traveled together, visiting and establishing churches. *Paul and Barnabas appointed elders for them in each church and, with prayer and fasting, committed them to the Lord in whom they had put their trust* (Acts 14:23).

The forty-day fasts of Moses and Jesus were supernatural fasts, not examples to be followed. The human body can't normally survive without water more than a few days. Both Jesus and Daniel overcame the enemy because of their extended fasts.

Daniel recorded a partial fast. *"At that time I, Daniel, mourned for three weeks. I ate no choice food; no meat or wine touched my lips; and I used no lotions at all until the three weeks were over* (Daniel 10:3).

NOT A CURE-ALL

"Fasting is neither a gimmick nor a cure-all. God does not deal in such things. God has made full provision for the total well-being of His people in every area of their lives—spiritual, physical, and material. Fasting is one part of this total provision. Fasting is not a substitute for any other part of God's provision. Conversely, no other part of God's provision is a substitute for fasting."[2]

If something is outside the will of God, fasting will not put it in God's will. God's righteous judgment on David's sinful acts of adultery and murder was not changed by his seven days of fasting. The fast changed David.

AMERICA FASTS

America has a long history of observing days of prayer and fasting. The Continental Congress proclaimed the first national day of prayer and fasting in 1776 that God might bless the land. Twice each year until 1783 national days of prayer and fasting were observed.

President Lincoln declared a day of humiliation, prayer, and fasting on three separate occasions, beginning April 30, 1863, and during the Civil War. Congress designated November 24, 1885, as a national day of fasting to raise funds to combat hunger. President Reagan repeated it in 1985 for the same reason.

BEGINNING TO FAST

Don't begin with a long period of fasting. Begin by omitting one or two meals and gradually move on to longer periods, such as a day or two. Remember fasting is always linked with prayer. Abstaining from food to lose weight is not true fasting. Read portions of Scripture and tailor your prayers around them. The Psalms are especially good for this. If you chose to avoid all solid food, drinking clear liquids will eliminate some of the unpleasant effects that can come with fasting.

God is limited only from the human side. He is always willing to give beyond our asking if the human conditions He has so plainly laid down in His Word are fulfilled. Those who are most ready to trust God without other evidence than His Word always receive the greatest number of visible evidences.

Fasting can be Abused

"Fasting is any deliberate self-denial, an abstinence for the purpose of becoming spiritually stronger and advancing the work of the kingdom of God."[3] We must examine our motives when we choose to fast. We don't fast to earn God's blessing or to impress others. God makes it clear in Isaiah 58:1-11 that our fasting should never be a substitute for obedience.

In his excellent book, *Touch the World through Prayer*, Wesley Duewel offers a list titled "How to Fast unto the Lord."[4]

1. Fast to please the Lord—because you want to draw nearer to Him.
2. Fast in response to God's call.
3. Fast to humble yourself before God.
4. Fast to seek God's face more fully. Fasting is a sacred way to seek God with all your heart.
5. Fast as a holy discipline of your soul.

"Remember that the apostolic methods are still valid today. Satan hates fasting, but God honors fasting. In this missionary age in which a militant church must win strategic battles for the Lord, accept again God's strategy of adding fasting to prayer."[5]

Your Personal Prayer Manual

Title the last divider in your prayer manual "Faith and Fasting." On one page collect scriptures from your daily reading that encourage your faith. On the second page add scriptures showing examples of fasting and God's response. On a third page record your own times of fasting. Make complete records of your motives and God's answer. If your faith is weak it will be strengthened when you read your own history of answered prayers as they relate to fasting.

Examine Yourself

1. How does my faith rate: none, little, much, great?
2. What can be done to increase my faith?
3. When was the last time I fasted for spiritual reasons?
4. Am I convinced that fasting is important?
5. What am I reading or watching that keeps me from spending time reading the Bible to increase my faith?

Merciful Father, I thank You for Your gift of faith. Thank You for the opportunity to continually increase my faith by spending time in Your matchless Word. Help me discover, believe, and stand on Your promises. Thank You that I can partner with You through my prayers. Forgive me for not using my time more wisely in a way that will affect eternity in the lives of those You have placed around me. Enable me to hear You as You prompt me to fast and pray. Help me remove distractions from my time with You. I desire to please You in all I do, speak, and think. I pray in the name of Jesus my Lord. Amen.

"No one can become an authentic Christian on a steady diet of activity. Power comes out of stillness; strength comes out of solitude. Decisions that change the entire course of your life come out of the Holy of Holies, your times of stillness before God."[6]

—Bill Hybels

CHAPTER SIXTEEN

Final Words

For years I prayed, "God, give me the gift of organization." Like the tin man in the *Wizard of Oz,* who went searching for a heart only to discover he already had one, I took a good look at myself. The evidence confirmed I had the gift I yearned for. The *Jumpstart to Power Prayers* manual that you and I have created is one of the results.

USING YOUR PRAYER MANUAL

I am convinced God is pleased when we increase the scope and effectiveness of our prayers. Your prayer manual looks bare now, but with frequent contributions from your Bible reading and prayer time it will grow and bear much fruit. Depending on the time you make available, there are several ways you can use your manual. If you methodically focus on only one segment a day, you will visit each section twice a month. Or you can rely on the prompting of the Holy Spirit to lead you to a special portion for concentrated prayer. Be faithful and patient. Soon you will have a wonderful record of answered prayers that will greatly increase your faith. Answered prayers are strong motivators.

After I add a person's name to a specific subject, I add the day's date. If there is an urgent need for concentrated petition, there's also a page at the front of my manual for current urgent needs.

When I revisit a page with several names, I may pray for each one again, or I may place my hand over all the names and pray for the group. I always thank God for His answers, even those that are not yet evident.

If you are in the habit of journaling each day, you may wish to add pages for your journal after the final divider.

REMEMBER YOUR ENEMIES

Did you notice there is no separate segment for your enemies? In the section on intercession we are called to pray for them, also. If they haven't been included on appropriate pages, take the time now to give some thought to their needs and put them in your manual. Wonderful things will happen to them and to you when you are praying for your enemies.

WHEN GOD IS SILENT

The mystery of seemingly unanswered prayers can discourage us. Sometimes I have grown weary of praying for the same thing over and over. I want to shout, "God, why don't you fix that?"

There are several reasons why we don't always see answers immediately. Remember that God has given each of us free will. The person we are praying for may have personal problems and sin that is blocking God's blessing. It might be inappropriate for God to answer our prayer the way we hope. It may not be the right time. In short, God always answers our prayers. His answers include *yes, no,* and *not now.* But we should never be guilty of neglecting to pray. We must trust God that His timing is perfect.

James 4:2 gives us one answer. *You do not have because you do not ask God. When you ask, you do not receive, because you ask with wrong motives, that you may spend what you get on your pleasures.*

166

PRAYERS, THE INCENSE OF HEAVEN

The book of Revelation gives us a beautiful picture of our prayers in heaven. *And when He (the Lamb) had taken it, the four living creatures and the twenty-four elders fell down before the Lamb. Each one had a harp and they were holding golden bowls full of incense, which are the prayers of the saints (Revelation 5:8). Another angel, who had a golden censer, came and stood at the altar. He was given much incense to offer, with the prayers of all the saints, on the golden altar before the throne. The smoke of the incense, together with the prayers of the saints, went up before God from the angel's hand* (Revelation 8:3-4).

OTHER RESOURCES

We have only briefly studied each of the subjects included in the prayer manual. There are valuable exhaustive studies written by learned scholars on each of these subjects. I have been guilty of spending more time reading about prayer than I spent in prayer. Dr. Seuss comments in one of his rhymes that there's so much to be read it's impossible to cram all those words in our head. I hope *Jumpstart to Power Prayers* will prevent you from repeating my mistake, i.e., spending more time reading about prayer than praying. God's Word is the best prayer resource we have.

A jumpstart is a surge of power to put a dead battery into action again. We certainly aren't dead batteries, but each of us *has* felt a need to be recharged from time to time. My prayer is that you will allow God's incomparable Word to jumpstart your prayers and lead you as the Holy Spirit directs.

THE END IS JUST THE BEGINNING

- We have affirmed the big picture of God's plan and desire for our prayers.
- We have determined the power for our prayers is found in God's Word.

- We have created a personal prayer manual that is barely begun. It will become your jumpstart to powerful prayers.

Your relationship with the Lord Jesus will become one of greater intimacy and trust as your prayer manual grows. Though mountains will be moved and enemies put to flight, more will come to take their place. You will experience a fuller level of what Jesus meant when he said, *"I have come that they may have life, and have it to the full"* (John 10:10).

Someone once said, "If you would work *for* God, form a committee; if you would work *with* God, you must pray."

Hudson Taylor, a man who devoted himself to obtaining his provisions from God, not man, said this about prayer: "The power of prayer cannot be diminished by distance; it is not limited by age, infirmity, or daily duty; political changes and restrictions cannot alter its effectiveness; for the Word still stands, 'If ye shall ask anything in my name I will do it.' The power of prayer in the life of an obedient Christian can only be undermined by neglect."[1]

Holy God, who am I that You invite me to enter Your throne room and intercede not just for family and friends, but also for nations and those in positions of power? Thank You that You give me not what I deserve, but what I don't deserve. Thank You for making me a joint-heir with Jesus. Thank You for Your mercy and love. Lord, give me a praying heart and a listening ear. Continue to teach me to pray. Teach me to discipline my life, making prayer a first priority. May my praise and worship be pleasing to You. I come to You in the precious name of Your beloved Son, Jesus. Amen.

Endnotes

Letter to Readers

1. George W. Bush, Remarks on National Day of Prayer, May 4, 2006.

Chapter One: The Power Connection

1. Basil Miller, *George Muller, Man of Faith & Miracles* (Minneapolis, Minnesota: Dimension Books, Bethany Fellowship, Inc., 1941), 108.
2. M. Basilea Schlink, *Realities* (Grand Rapids, Michigan: Zondervan Publishing House, 1966), 133.

Chapter Two: The Call to Action

1. B. J. Willhite, "Why Pray," Charisma & Christian Life, January 1989, 69.
2. Miller.
3. Miller, 108.
4. Miller, 115.
5. Dr. and Mrs. Howard Taylor, *Hudson Taylor's Spiritual Secret* (Chicago: Moody Press), 32.
6. Rosalind Goforth, *Climbing* (Elkhart, Indiana: Bethel Publishing), 94.

7. Rosalind Goforth, *How I Know God Answers Prayer* (Lincoln, Nebraska: Back to the Bible Publishers), 43.
8. Dr. Paul Yonggi Cho, *The Fourth Dimension Volume Two* (So. Plainfield, New Jersey: Bridge Publishing, Inc.,1983) xiii.
9. Gary Bergel, President, Intercessors for America.

Chapter Three: Get Better Acquainted with God

1. Jack W. Hayford, *Prayer is Invading the Impossible* (Plainfield, New Jersey: Logos International, 1977), 77.

Chapter Four: Spiritual Circuit Breakers

1. Schlink, 29.
2. Schlink, 31.
3. Schlink, 32.
4. Dr. Norman Vincent Peale, *Positive Imaging* (Old Tappan, New Jersey: Fleming H. Revell Co., 1982), 58.

Chapter Five: Personal Growth

1. Cho, 21.
2. An Unknown Author, *The kneeling Christian* (Grand Rapids, Michigan: Zondervan Publishing House 1945), 22,23.
3. Cho, 16.
4. David Wilkerson, *Beyond The Cross and the Switchblade* (Old Tappan, New Jersey: Fleming H. Revell Co., 1974), 24.
5. George A Buttrick, *The Power of Prayer Today* (Waco, Texas: Word Books, 1970), 46.

Chapter Six: Called to Intercede

1. Wesley L Duewel, *Touch the World through Prayer* (Grand Rapids, Michigan: Francis Asbury Press, 1986), 11.
2. Paul E. Billheimer, *Destined for the Throne* (Minneapolis, Minnesota: Bethany House Publishers, 1983), 40.
3. Corrie ten Boom, *In My Father's House* (Old Tappan, New Jersey: Fleming H. Revell Co., 1976), 24, 25.
4. Billheimer, 52.
5. Duewel, 254, 255.

6. Judson Cornwall, *Praying the Scriptures* (Creation House, Lake Mary, FL 1990), 43.

Chapter 7: Standing in the Generation Gap

1. Dean Sherman *Spiritual Warfare for Every Christian* (YWAM Publishing, Seattle, WA, 1990), 160.

Chapter Eight: Into the Harvest Fields

1. Miller, 145.
2. Miller, 146.
3. ten Boom, 23, 24.
4. Dr. Robert C. Frost, *Aglow with the Spirit* (Plainfield, New Jersey: Logos International, 1971), 73.

Chapter Nine: Equipped to Harvest

1. James Gilchrist Lawson, *Deeper Experiences of Famous Christians,* (Warner Press, Anderson, IN, 1970, © 1911), 9.
2. Lawson, 8.
3. David Wilkerson, *The Cross and the Switchblade,* (Fleming H. Revell Company: Old Tappan, NJ, 1962).
4. David Wilkerson newsletter, August 13, 1990.
5. Hayford, 67.

Chapter Ten: Workers in the Harvest

1. The Jesus Film Project, (P.O. Box 72007, San Clemente, CA 92674-2007; www.jesusfilm.org).
2. The Jesus Film Project, Jim Green letter, April 3, 2006.
3. Trinity Broadcasting Network, Newsletter, January 2006 (P.O. Box A, Santa Ana, CA 92711; www.tbn.org).
4. Trinity Broadcasting Network, Newsletter, March 2006.
5. Prison Fellowship, Mark Early letter, January 3, 2006 (P.O. Box 1550, Merrifield, VA 22116-1550; www.pfi.org).
6. Book of Hope, Global Report, January 2006 (3111 S.W. 10th St., Pompano FL 33069; www.bookofhope.net).

7. Open Doors USA, Dr. Carl Moeller letter, April 13, 2006 (P.O. Box 27001, Santa Ana, CA 92799; www.opendoorsusa.org).
8. Schlink, 71.
9. C. Peter Wagner, *Prayer Shield* (Venture, CA: Regal Books, 1992), 181.

Chapter 11: The Nation and Those in Authority

1. Open Doors USA, newsletter, November 1990.
2. Norman P. Grubb, *Rees Howells Intercessor* (Christian Literature Crusade, Fort Washington, Pennsylvania, 19034), 247.
3. Grubb, 261-262.
4. www.ronaldreagan.com, Courtesy of Simon & Shuster.
5. Intercessors for America (P.O. Box 915, Purcellville, VA 20134; www.ifapray.org).
6. American Center for Law and Justice (P.O. Box 90555, Washington, D.C. 20090-0555; www.aclj.org).
7. American Family Association (P.O. Drawer 2440, Tupelo, MI 38803; www.afa.net).
8. Institute of Basic Life Principles (www.billgothard.com). Used by permission.
9. Ken Blue, *Authority to Heal* (Intervarsity Press, Downers Grove, IL 60515, 1987), 40.

Chapter 12: Healing and Wholeness

1. Blue, 31.
2. Sherman, 186.

Chapter 13: Deliver Us from Evil

1. C. S. Lewis, *The Screwtape Letters* (The Macmillan Co, New York, 1962), viii.
2. Duewel, 119.
3. Sherman, 124,125.
4. Sherman, 186.

5. Corrie ten Boom, *Defeated Enemies* (Christian Literature Crusade, Ft. Washington, PA, 1970), 11.
6. Dr. Ed Murphy, *The Handbook for Spiritual Warfare* (Thomas Nelson Publisher, Inc, Nashville, NT, 1992), 578.
7. Billheimer, 15.

Chapter 14: Setting Prisoners Free

1. Charles W. Colson, *Born Again* (Chosen Books, Old Tappan, NJ) 1976. Quote from Book Jacket, Catherine Marshall.
2. Cornwall, 41.

Chapter 15: Faith and Fasting

1. Gordon Lindsay, *Prayer and Fasting, The Master Key to the Impossible* (Christ for the Nations, Inc, Dallas, TX, 1977), 15.
2. Derek Prince, *Shaping History through Prayer and Fasting* (Fleming H. Revell Co., Old Tappan, NJ, 1973), 87.
3. Duewel, 98.
4. Duewel, 100.
5. Duewel, 102.
6. Bill Hybels, *Too Busy Not to Pray* (Intervarsity Press, Downers Grove, IL, 1988), 120.

Chapter 16: Final Words

1. Hudson Taylor, *To China with Love* (Dimension Books, Bethany Fellowship, Inc., Minneapolis, MN, 17th edition), 159.

Printed in the United States
65441LVS00002B/241-459

PC 3/25/07